Lithuanians in Michigan

DISCOVERING THE PEOPLES OF MICHIGAN

Arthur W. Helweg, Russell M. Magnaghi, and Linwood H. Cousins, *Series Editors*

Ethnicity in Michigan: Issues and People
Jack Glazier and Arthur W. Helweg

African Americans in Michigan
Lewis Walker, Benjamin C. Wilson,
and Linwood H. Cousins

Albanians in Michigan
Frances Trix

Amish in Michigan
Gertrude Enders Huntington

Arab Americans in Michigan
Rosina J. Hassoun

Asian Indians in Michigan
Arthur W. Helweg

Belgians in Michigan
Bernard A. Cook

Chaldeans in Michigan
Mary C. Sengstock

Copts in Michigan
Eliot Dickinson

Cornish in Michigan
Russell M. Magnaghi

Dutch in Michigan
Larry ten Harmsel

Finns in Michigan
Gary Kaunonen

French Canadians in Michigan
John P. DuLong

Germans in Michigan
Jeremy W. Kilar

Greeks in Michigan
Stavros K. Frangos

Hungarians in Michigan
Éva V. Huseby-Darvas

Irish in Michigan
Seamus P. Metress and Eileen K. Metress

Italians in Michigan
Russell M. Magnaghi

Jews in Michigan
Judith Levin Cantor

Latinos in Michigan
David A. Badillo

Latvians in Michigan
Silvija D. Meija

Lithuanians in Michigan
Marius K. Grazulis

Mexicans and Mexican Americans in Michigan
Rudolph Valier Alvarado
and Sonya Yvette Alvarado

Poles in Michigan
Dennis Badaczewski

Scandinavians in Michigan
Jeffrey W. Hancks

Scots in Michigan
Alan T. Forrester

South Slavs in Michigan
Daniel Cetinich

Yankees in Michigan
Brian C. Wilson

Discovering the Peoples of Michigan is a series of publications examining the state's rich multicultural heritage. The series makes available an interesting, affordable, and varied collection of books that enables students and educated lay readers to explore Michigan's ethnic dynamics. A knowledge of the state's rapidly changing multicultural history has far-reaching implications for human relations, education, public policy, and planning. We believe that Discovering the Peoples of Michigan will enhance understanding of the unique contributions that diverse and often unrecognized communities have made to Michigan's history and culture.

Lithuanians in Michigan

Marius K. Grazulis

Michigan State University Press

East Lansing

♾ The paper used in this publication meets the minimum requirements
of ANSI/NISO Z39.48-1992 (R 1997) (Permanence of Paper).

Michigan State University Press
East Lansing, Michigan 48823-5245

Printed and bound in the United States of America.

15   14   13   12   11   10   09   1   2   3   4   5   6   7   8   9   10

ISBN: 978-0-87013-813-3

LIBRARY OF CONGRESS CATALOGING-IN-PUBLICATION DATA
Grazulis, Marius K.
Lithuanians in Michigan / Marius K. Grazulis.
p. cm.—(Discovering the peoples of Michigan)
Includes bibliographical references and index.
ISBN 978-0-87013-813-3 (pbk. : alk. paper) 1. Lithuanian Americans—Michigan—History.
2. Immigrants—Michigan—History. 3. Lithuanian Americans—Michigan—Social life and customs.
4. Michigan—Ethnic relations. 5. Michigan—Social life and customs. 6. Michigan—
Emigration and immigration. 7. Lithuania—Emigration and immigration. I. Title.
F575.L7G73 2009
977.4'0049192—dc22
2008029581

Cover design by Ariana Grabec-Dingman
Book design by Sharp Des!gns, Lansing, Michigan
Cover photo is of campers with their counselor at Camp Dainava in Manchester, Michigan, in 2003.
Photo taken by Juozas Vaiciunas, from the author's personal collection.

Michigan State University Press is a member of the Green Press Initiative and is
committed to developing and encouraging ecologically responsible publishing
practices. For more information about the Green Press Initiative and the use of
recycled paper in book publishing, please visit *www.greenpressinitiative.org*.

Visit Michigan State University Press on the World Wide Web at *www.msupress.msu.edu*

*For my parents
and Dr. Robert Citino*

Contents

Introduction 1

Lithuanian History as a Background to Immigration 3

The First and Second Waves of Lithuanians in Michigan 7

Religion and Culture in the First and Second Waves 17

Lithuanians and Sports 39

The Third and Fourth Waves of Lithuanian Immigration to Michigan. ... 45

Politics 57

The Fourth Wave 63

The Fifth Wave of Immigration and Today 65

The Union Pier Experience 71

The Future of Lithuanians in Michigan 77

Conclusion 79

SIDEBARS

Bishop Salatka of Marquette 24

Old Country Farmer's Cheese 33

Lithuanian Jews 36

Louis Getz 37

Milda's Corner Store 73

APPENDICES

Appendix 1. Lithuanian Recipes 81
Appendix 2. Lithuanian Organizations 83

Notes... 85
For Further Reference 91
Index... 97

Introduction

In Lithuanian "Saturday School" at the Lithuanian Cultural Center in Southfield, high school students learned a poem, *Čičinskas* (pronounced "chi-CHIN-skas"), written by Maironis in 1907. Čičinskas is a prince eager for power in renaissance Lithuania. In order for Čičinskas to get his power he has to betray his homeland. Because he has betrayed his homeland, a lightning bolt kills him and his estate sinks into the ground. Every time people bury him, the ground spits him out. Ultimately, his body is taken away to a distant land and nobody knows what happens to it. The high school students were told that the moral of the story is that one should not forget, betray, or forsake one's homeland or God will return the misdeed with some kind of damnation. The author wrote this poem when many of his compatriots were leaving for the New World in the late 1800s and early 1900s. Maironis was obviously trying to discourage them from leaving Lithuania. If they left, he wanted them to heed his warning not to forget the homeland. Since Maironis's time, five waves of Lithuanian immigrants have arrived in the United States and, for the most part, each successive wave has become assimilated. Over a century and a half, immigrant Lithuanians have struggled to keep their identity in the New World and to organize themselves in the hopes of slowing the assimilation process.

Lithuanian culture in the world, much less the United States or Michigan, is not very well known because of the small number of Lithuanians. Lithuania's population in the twentieth century never exceeded four million. Despite the small numbers in Lithuania and those immigrating at one time or another, they have started a community in every region of Michigan and have come to work in many major industries of Michigan. The number of Lithuanians in Michigan is small compared to other areas of the United States, like Chicago and the Pennsylvania anthracite coal region. Yet, because of its central location among the Lithuanian colonies of the Midwest, Michigan has played an important role for Lithuanians throughout the United States over the years.

A pattern has evolved through the waves of immigration. Just as the last wave of Lithuanian organization and culture is in decline, the new wave of immigrants (except for the fourth wave of immigration) reinvigorates the Lithuanian community in Michigan. The cost of mixing the old wave of immigrants with the new wave is a cultural dissonance between the two. Even today, the misunderstanding between fifth wave immigrants, those who have arrived since the independence of Lithuania from the Soviet Union in 1990, and third wave immigrants, those who immigrated between 1945 and 1955, has created a cultural dissonance. Each wave tends to congregate at an established Lithuanian parish, but each wave tends to create their own social organizations separate from those of the previous wave of immigrants. This phenomenon has made an impact on Lithuanians in Michigan.

Lithuanian History as a Background to Immigration

To understand the variables impacting Lithuanian immigration to Michigan in the 1860s, one must understand the geopolitical realities of Lithuania in medieval Europe. Geographically, Lithuania has generally held its ethnogeographic boundaries since the year 1000. Without the port of Klaipėda (Memel in German), its fifty-mile coast on the Baltic Sea would be reduced to a handful of miles. Besides its small coast, in medieval times Lithuania was landlocked by huge, dense forests. With only one waterway, the Nemunas River (the Nieman River, in German), leading inland and no valuable resources, the country was not considered by invaders to be worth the struggle to fight through the forest and then a Lithuanian army on the other side. This is a major reason why Lithuanians were the last Europeans to be Christianized. The Lithuanian state finally unified itself in the 1200s in reaction to the Livonian Order (geographically Latvia today) and the Teutonic Order (which became known as Prussia, but is called the Kaliningrad Region today) trying to Christianize Lithuania. Ultimately, the enemies on all sides forced Lithuanians to actively fight the aggression. Lithuania fought with much success. The Lithuanian Empire under Vytautas (Witold) the Great in the early 1400s reached its largest geographic extent. Its borders reached from near Moscow in the east to Poland in the west and from Novgorod in the north to the Black Sea in the south. Of course, the population was not ethnically Lithuanian,

The Republic of Lithuania since its independence from the Soviet Union in 1990.

because empires of this kind were created through military invasion or alliance. As one can see, Lithuanians have always had to interact with Russians, Germans, and Poles.

Lithuania, despite fiercely defending its pagan culture, became a Roman Catholic state because of political realities. To defeat the Teutonic invasion, Vytautas the Great made an alliance with his first cousin, King Jogaila of Poland (Jogiella, in Polish). In the epic battle at Tannenburg (Žalgiris in Lithuanian) in 1410, the Polish/Lithuanian alliance defeated the Teutonic Order and prevented any invasion of Lithuania by the Teutonic Order. This Polish-Lithuanian alliance had a huge impact on the Lithuanian culture for centuries to come. The alliance became an official state order through the

Union of Lublin in 1569. The Grand Duchy of Lithuania and the Polish Kingdom became equal political partners through one state. Unfortunately, there was no cultural equality. The Lithuanian culture was considered the epitome of the backward peasant life.[1] Lithuanian royalty and landowners used the Polish language and with time ignored the Lithuanian language. The royalty lost their connection to the average Lithuanian. In time, Poles saw the Lithuanians as unenlightened Poles, when in fact they were two separate ethnicities. Linguists have confirmed this by the separation of the two in language. Although both are from the Indo-European family of languages, the Polish language is a part of the Slavic branch, while Lithuanian is Baltic. (The only other language in the Baltic branch is Latvian.)

While language and culture split the Poles and Lithuanians, another sociological entity held them together: Roman Catholicism. The Lithuanians, while still holding on to pagan beliefs, slowly became Roman Catholic. Polish priests went into Lithuania in the Middle Ages and converted the Lithuanian pagans to Catholicism. What the Teutonic Knights could not accomplish by sword, the Poles accomplished through alliance. Today, Lithuanians worldwide are overwhelmingly Roman Catholic. Despite the linguistic and cultural dispute, the glue of Catholicism created a dynamic relationship between Lithuanians and Polish immigrants coming to the United States.

After years of political and geographic recession caused by Swedish, Austrian, Prussian, and Russian encroachments, by 1795 Lithuania and Poland did not formally exist. The Third Partition between the Russian Empire, the Austrian-Hungarian Empire, and the Prussian Empire condemned Poland-Lithuania into seemingly historical oblivion. All of Lithuania fell under the rule of the Russian Empire.

Russian rule was harsh for Lithuanians. The tsar declared a cultural war on Lithuania in an attempt to russify it. Lithuanian private schools were shut down because they taught Lithuanian language and culture, as opposed to Russian, which was taught in the public schools. Most importantly, the only Lithuanian university at that time, the Vilnius University, was closed in 1832 for revolutionary activity during the uprisings in 1831. The Lithuanian Latin alphabet was replaced by the Cyrillic (the Russian alphabet) phonetic equivalent in 1864. Lithuanian men were forced to serve a twenty-five-year conscription period in the czarist army. The tsar's advisor in Lithuania tried to wipe away the Lithuanian culture and language from the people's memory.

Consequences to this cultural war were many. With the idea of nationalism running wild in Europe, a Lithuanian cultural renewal from the grassroots created a backlash to these anti-Lithuanian policies. Peasants began teaching the Lithuanian language in the Latin alphabet to their children at home. Lithuanian book smugglers from Tilžė (Tilsit in German), a city controlled by Prussia across the Nemunas River, infiltrated the countryside with the help of Lithuanian parish priests, like Maironis. Many of the books were bankrolled and even printed in the United States by Lithuanian-Americans. In the end, the Lithuanian cultural backlash resulted in the political goal of independence. The movement gained a lot of momentum from Lithuanians in the United States starting in the 1890s. Independence was finally achieved in 1918. Another consequence to the tsar's cultural war was the first wave of immigrants to the United States and Michigan. A trickle of Lithuanians came to the United States in the 1860s and to Michigan in the 1870s in reaction to negative tsarist economic and social policies in Lithuania.

The First and Second Waves of Lithuanians in Michigan

The first wave of Lithuanian immigrants came to the United States beginning in 1860. This wave ended in 1918, near the end of World War I, with the creation of the Lithuanian republic. The difference between the first and second waves of Lithuanians coming to the United States and Michigan is slight. The emigrating agent changed from tsarist Russian to independent Lithuanian, meaning the cultural reasons for leaving Lithuania disappeared. However, the economic reasons for leaving Lithuania continued. Therefore, the first and second waves of Lithuanian immigration will be generally treated as one and the same in this study.

Genealogists and historians have a difficult, if not impossible, task in trying to identify Lithuanians in the census data prior to 1920. The first problem would be the problem of determining "country of origin." As mentioned, Lithuania was a part of tsarist Russia. Therefore, when immigrants declared where they had originated, many wrote down Russia, even though they came from a Lithuanian village. Knowing Lithuanian geography helps in this endeavor, because the village or city of birth was documented on the 1920 United States Census. In fact, the United States Census did not recognize the ethnicity of "Lithuanian" until 1899. But even then, one must be careful because Lithuanian minorities lived throughout the area near the borders of Lithuania in the cities and villages of Poland, Russia, Latvia, and Prussia.

A Lithuanian immigrant documenting he was from Minsk, Lida, Grodno, or Naugard, Russia, coming to Michigan could very well have been the first Lithuanian to live in Michigan.

Another problem with determining the country of origin is the fear associated with immigrating. Many Lithuanians leaving their homeland left illegally, according to tsarist laws, which did not recognize emigration. Therefore, if one left Lithuania for another country without a permit or visa, then one could be punished. Punishment was not severe. Arrest, interrogation, and release were the norm. Agents (like the "coyotes" in the American southwest today) agitating, organizing, and leading the illegal emigrants faced the more severe penalties of prosecution and exile. Out of fear of repatriation, many Lithuanians wrote down a country of origin other than Russia. Usually, origin of emigration was given as Prussia or Germany. This is not surprising, since most of the immigration business in Lithuania was done through German agents. The agents in Lithuania, more often than not, worked for the Hamburg-America Line or the North German Lloyd. The agents most often got the emigrants to Bremen or Hamburg for transportation to the United States.[2] Lithuanians easily could write down Prussia or Germany as their country of origin, since the only documentation they did have was steamship tickets from Germany. The first Lithuanian to live in Michigan could have documented him- or herself as German or Prussian.

Another problem with searching for Lithuanian roots is the spelling of names. As stated previously, Lithuanians were russified in the 1800s, and had been polonized since the 1500s. Therefore the names of Lithuanians found in directories could be spelled to reflect a misleading Polish or Russian background. A Lithuanian name like "Rinkevičius" would be polonized into "Rinkevicz," or "Šatkauskas" into "Shatkowski," and "Radinovičius" russified into "Radinovich."

Upon entering the United States, Lithuanian names were also changed by immigration officials. Many reasons account for this. First, names were sometimes misspelled since foreign names with foreign spellings weren't the easiest to transcribe. These were honest mistakes. Officials also wrote the English phonetic equivalent for Lithuanian names. Some names were purposely changed to be either shorter or anglicized. This made work easier for the bureaucracy and, more than likely, made life easier for the immigrant (but more difficult for future historians and genealogists). Immigrants also changed or shortened their name to reflect the Anglo culture around them. The author Ed Gillis writes that his family's name was changed to reflect a Welsh background from the Lithuanian "Gylys" (pronounced "gee-lees" with a hard "g" as in "good").[3] "Lucas" could be the shortened and anglicized version of "Lukasevičius" or "Lukauskas."

Lithuanian women who married into another ethnic group would also be a problem in tracking Lithuanians in Michigan. Possibly the first Lithuanian in Michigan was the wife of some Polish, Russian, German, or Latvian immigrant. She took her husband's name and we would have no record of her maiden name, and yet she would be the first Lithuanian to live in Michigan. Because Lithuanian names were changed for many different reasons, historians and genealogists will always have problems finding these early Lithuanian immigrants.

The first Lithuanian to live in Michigan is an elusive distinction. One source claims a picture exists of a hundredth anniversary of Lithuanian families that settled in Grand Rapids. This supposedly proves that families like the Galinis, Čiplis, Bendžiūnas, and Zygmantus arrived in the 1860s.[4] Edward Gillis writes that the Grand Rapids directories in the 1870s list names like Brinkus and Koshauska, but no other evidence exists to prove their descent. He writes that the first provable Lithuanian in Grand Rapids was a laborer named Louis Galinis listed in the 1884–86 city directory as living on Hamilton Avenue in the heart of what would become Lithuanian Town.[5] A. Misiukonis is named as the first to live in Detroit in 1872, followed by the Salasevičius and Kasevičius families in the late 1880s.[6] These families, whether in Grand Rapids or Detroit, represent the first of many Lithuanians to come through five waves of immigration.

If population movement was a coin, then it is made of two sides: Emigration on one side and immigration on the other. Lithuanians at first came to the United States at a trickle, but soon their immigration became a flood. The first Lithuanians to emigrate came after the disastrous crop failures of the late 1860s. About a thousand Lithuanians a year emigrated to the United States. By 1899, the annual average immigration rate was almost 3,000. A deluge of Lithuanian immigration started in 1905 when the United States received 18,604 Lithuanians, followed by 14,257 in 1906, and 25,884 in 1907. These numbers decreased but rose again on the eve of World War I, with 14,071 Lithuanians immigrating to the United States in 1912, 24,647 in 1913,

Thomasma Brothers Rein and Walter, meat market, 1895. Courtesy of the Grand Rapids History and Special Collections, Archives, Grand Rapids Public Library, Grand Rapids, Michigan.

and 21,584 in 1914.[7] Estimates put 55,000 Lithuanians immigrating to the United States before 1899 and 252,594 between 1899 and 1914. The total figure would be 307,594 Lithuanian immigrants to the United States between 1860 and 1914. These figures are staggering for a country like Lithuania with a population as low as 1.6 million in the late 1800s.

The second wave of Lithuanian emigration lasted from roughly 1918 until 1940. Interestingly, people were still leaving Lithuania at the same rate as in the first wave, but immigrating to parts of the world other than the United States. Lithuanian immigration to the United States declined at this time because of immigration quotas set by law in the United States in 1921. The quota was set at 3 percent of the American immigration population from the 1920 Census. According to this law, 344 Lithuanians could legally immigrate to the United States each year. Those who were naturalized and re-immigrating and family members from Lithuania who were immigrating to join a naturalized immigrant in the United States were not counted as part of the quota. The quota was raised to 366 in 1929. Even so, 22,325 Lithuanians immigrated to the United States between 1920 and 1923. Immigration decreased to roughly 1,000 a year for the rest of the 1920s.[8] By 1930, with the world in economic depression and no need for cheap labor, Lithuanians did not immigrate in large numbers.

With so many leaving their homeland in these first two waves, the question surfaces: Why did Lithuanians leave Lithuania at this time? Some Lithuanians may have left because of the tsarist social repression alone, but, coupled with economic deprivation, the disposition to emigrate became strong. Not very well known are the economic reasons behind emigration. Nineteenth-century Lithuania was one of the least developed areas in Europe. While the rest of Europe built railroads and factories for mass production, Lithuania was left to its old agrarian, feudalist ways. As a part of the Russian Empire, Lithuania averaged 48 heavy industry workers per 10,000 citizens, compared to the rest of the Russian *guberniyas* (governing districts), which had 186 workers.

Despite the freedom given to serfs in 1861, in the late nineteenth century 66 percent of the population of Lithuania were farm workers, who did not own land. Jews, Poles, and Russians dominated work in the cities, leaving Lithuanian farmhands looking for work but unable to find it. In effect, Lithuania had a huge labor surplus, which could not be kept employed at a just wage. Between 1883 and 1888 the average Lithuanian male farmhand in the Suwalki *guberniya* made about 42 kopecks a day (a kopeck is equivalent to the American cent). This ranked forty-fourth in the Russian Empire. For further comparison, in 1890, the average Russian farmhand earned $2.88 a week, meaning Lithuanian farmhands were clearly competing in a surplus market in the Lithuanian *guberniyas.* The polar opposite was true in the United States, with a $9.00 to $10.50 weekly wage for a farmhand.[9] In short, American farmhands made three to four times more money each week than the average Lithuanian farmhand.

When famine occurred in 1867–68, young Lithuanians had no choice but to leave their homeland in order to survive. Lithuanians thus left their homes for a better living, as well as in response to russification and conscription.

The other side of the population movement coin is immigration. Why would a Lithuanian choose to immigrate to the United States of America, and specifically to Michigan? The answer is a combination of geography and economics. Lithuanians chose to live in places where they could quickly find work at a better wage than in Lithuania. Not only did they find freedom from persecution in the United States, but they found "The American Dream."[10]

For the most part, Lithuanians in the 1800s overlooked Michigan as a place to colonize. Lithuanians stayed and worked on the East Coast in the 1870s, encouraged by the close proximity of unskilled employment. The Pennsylvanian anthracite coal region gave Lithuanian immigrants the first Lithuanian parishes, communities, and organizations. In 1899, 2,534 Lithuanians immigrated directly to Pennsylvania, compared to 3,881 immigrating to the East and Midwest.[11] By 1900, the Lithuanian population in Chicago was at 14,000 and the one in Pennsylvania dwarfed the Michigan Lithuanian population. At this time Detroit had approximately 400 Lithuanians and Grand Rapids only a handful.[12] By 1914, Michigan hosted 3,427 Lithuanians. This figure put Michigan ninth highest in the nation in terms of number of Lithuanians. Pennsylvania was first, followed by Illinois, then New York.[13] By 1920 Detroit had 2,653 Lithuanians, or three-quarters of those living in Michigan.[14]

Apparently, the lure of unskilled work at high wages drove Lithuanians to the industrial parts of Michigan. In the Grand Rapids furniture industry, workers were paid around 15 cents an hour, or $9.00 for a sixty-hour work week, in the 1910s. This was raised to 20 cents an hour in the 1920s.[15] The famous Ford five-dollar workdays in his Highland Park factory allowed for workers to make $300 for a sixty-hour work week in January of 1914. This doubled the wage from $2.50 a day or a $150 workweek in December of 1913.[16] Mining copper gave a worker in the Houghton area a $3.00 a day wage in 1914.[17] The comparison to the same unskilled industrial jobs in Russia from 1906 to 1913 is astounding. In St. Petersburg, the city in Russia with the highest wages, the average industrial worker earned 368 rubles a year. With the rate of exchange taken into account, the equivalent worker in the United States made an annual wage of 3,692 rubles![18] No wonder Lithuanians left their country and the countryside for industrialized cities in Michigan and around the world.

A study of data shows that many first- and second-wave Lithuanians sought work elsewhere before settling in Michigan. The largest number, unsurprisingly, came to Michigan from Pennsylvania's coal region, with a slightly smaller number coming from Illinois. The next largest group came from New York and New England. Others came from mining states not

Finishing Room, Imperial Furniture Company, 1930s. Courtesy of the Grand Rapids History and Special Collections, Archives, Grand Rapids Public Library, Grand Rapids, Michigan.

considered Lithuanian immigrant destinations: Montana (copper mining) and Alabama, Oklahoma, and Tennessee (coal mining). By tracing the birthplace of children, the erratic nature of employment for an immigrant becomes apparent. One Lithuanian family had their first child in Wisconsin, the next in Michigan, the third in Lithuania, and the final two in Michigan. A few exceptions show Lithuanians arriving to Michigan from foreign lands. One came by way of Brazil, while a few were first miners in England and Scotland before crossing the Atlantic.[19]

As Lithuanians moved to Michigan in the first two waves of immigration, what sociological characteristics did they most likely have? Lithuanians coming to Michigan are best characterized as agricultural, uneducated, poor males of working age. The agricultural characteristic has already been described. The fact that most of the Lithuanians moving to the United States initially were males of working age is not surprising. Most of these males were dodging the tsarist requirement of twenty-five years of military service. U.S. statistics concerning the 1899–1914 immigrants show a two to one ratio

of men to women coming from Lithuania.[20] Many of these males returned to
Lithuania to bring their families with them or, once they saved enough, paid
for their family to join them.

Lithuanians were more often than not illiterate. The tsarist war on Lithuania's culture led to many families forgoing public education and teaching
their children at home. The 1930 U.S. Census shows only a 48 percent reading
and writing rate among Lithuanian immigrants.[21] Among the immigrant ethnicities coming from Russia, Lithuanians were one of, if not the most illiterate group.[22] Despite the large numbers of Lithuanians in Detroit, Lithuanian
intellectuals did not come to Michigan. Intellectuals worked and agitated for
Lithuanian rights out of Chicago, Pennsylvania, or the Northeast. The major
Lithuanian-American intellectuals of the time, like Jonas Šliupas, Martynas
Yčas, Antanas Olišauskas, and Father Antanas Kaupas, all lived, worked, and
wrote in those areas of the United States. Detroit did not publish any Lithuanian newspapers or magazines, while New York and Chicago did.

Financially, Lithuanians were poor when they came to America and to
Michigan. Between 1899 and 1904, only 2,560 Lithuanians brought with them
$30 or more to the United States, while 47,456 brought less than $30. An immigrant brought an average amount of $13.40 during the time period of 1905
to 1909.[23]

During this period of Lithuanian population growth in Michigan, Lithuanians were mostly poor and could not buy farms or homes in the suburbs.
They moved to urban areas near factory work in Detroit and Grand Rapids.
An exception was the Lithuanian farming colony, known as Naujoji Lietuva
("New Lithuania"), that was established in Lake and Mason counties. These
farmers were already established immigrants who moved from the Chicago
area. They had the money to buy farms, but most Lithuanian immigrants
coming to Michigan had only enough money to find room and board and
start work.

Lithuanians, being uneducated, poor, and able-bodied males, were made
for Frederick Taylor's model of industry.[24] The Lithuanian immigrant exactly
fit the mold of the unskilled labor needed for mining, lumbering, and factory
work. Agrarian values gave Lithuanians the work ethic needed to toil on one
particular job for ten to twelve hours a day, six days a week. Being poverty-
stricken forced Lithuanians to stay on the job. Having an uneducated mind
allowed the company to mold the immigrant into what they needed.

Lithuanians at Ford Motor Company's Highland Park Plant in 1917 were a prime example. With 541 Lithuanians employed, they were the twelfth-largest ethnic group in the plant.[25] Using the 1920 Lithuanian population of Detroit, Lithuanians were one of the smaller ethnic groups in Detroit, ranking seventeenth.[26] One could conclude that Lithuanians in the Highland Park Plant were valued as employees, despite their poverty and ignorance. Many of these Lithuanians were reaching the $5 a day wage because of their work ethic. In order to receive this wage many requirements were put on the employee. An employee had to have a six months' residency in Detroit and six months of experience with Ford. Also, he must not send excessive amounts of salary abroad.[27] The ledger shows 427 Lithuanian employees having bank accounts at a total amount of $162,875, for an average savings of $381.44 per account.[28] The average would have been a considerable savings, equaling 76 workdays at $5 a day. Lithuanians were well on their way to becoming successful workers for Ford, because of their work ethic and the pressure to survive.

Religion and Culture in the First and Second Waves

Because of the low economic status of Lithuanians, they centered their social lives on the one thing they knew: culture. Lithuanian culture was focused on the Roman Catholic Church. If you go to Lithuania, the old Roman Catholic Churches are in the center of town. The local parish gave a sense of unity and, in many cases, defiance against the tsarist regime. The parish priest was considered a community leader and many times led the defiance, especially when the time came to smuggle in Latin alphabet Lithuanian books (many published in the United States by émigrés). The priest led the religious and educational life of the village. The same is true for the Lithuanian parishes and priests in Michigan during the first and second waves of immigration. Even today, the cultural activities of the Lithuanian communities in Detroit and Grand Rapids are centered around the Lithuanian parish.

The first Lithuanian churches in the United States began by breaking away from the Polish parish that Lithuanians would attend. Most Lithuanian priests at this time were trained in Polish seminaries, and as a result when they came to the United States they were assigned to Polish parishes. As Lithuanians immigrated, they moved near the Polish neighborhoods with a Lithuanian priest and would start a Lithuanian society within the Polish parish. Later, these societies would lead the movement to establish

Lithuanian parishes separate from the Polish ones. Of course, the Lithuanian priest made this possible. In some places in Pennsylvania, violence broke out between Poles and Lithuanians over this issue of separation, but not in Michigan.[29]

The next struggle for the Lithuanians was among themselves. After struggling to survive economically, Lithuanian immigrants became wary of sacrificing part of their wage to a church they did not own. According to Catholic rule, church property was deeded to the local bishop. To many Lithuanians, this meant they were giving their money to an Irish or German bishop, and that did not seem just. Lithuanian socialist nationalists like Jonas Šliupas and Antanas Olišauskas argued for independent Lithuanian parishes that were not under the local bishop's control. They argued that the parish had been the assimilating force in Lithuania ever since its arrival. The parish always led to polonization, and therefore, Lithuanians should separate themselves from this assimilating force.

Parish priests like Fathers Matas Kriaučiūnas and George Kolesinskis in Chicago maintained that being Lithuanian meant being Roman Catholic. The two are inseparable, and therefore people like the intellectual Šliupas were anti-Lithuanian, anti-Catholic, and thus immoral.[30] These struggles in places like Pennsylvania and Chicago did not take place in Michigan during the first and second waves (but a form of them between second- and third-wave immigrants took place in the 1970s, and another between third- and fifth-wave immigrants in the 1990s).

As in other places, Lithuanians first immigrated to Polish areas of Detroit, but also to German areas. Apparently half of the four hundred Lithuanians in Detroit in 1900 were Lutheran. Therefore they must have lived near the German area of Detroit.[31] The Catholics gravitated toward Polish areas of Detroit and Hamtramck. The Polish-Lithuanian relationship was cordial. By 1920 three Lithuanian parishes were created from these Polish neighborhoods.

All the parishes in Detroit had their beginnings with the first parish, St. George. A large concentration of Lithuanians lived near the Polish St. Albertus Church at Canfield and St. Aubin avenues. This was not far from St. Josephat (Polish) Church, where a Lithuanian priest, Fr. Casimir Valaitis, was an assistant. Lithuanians formed a St. George's Society to help Lithuanians worship in Lithuanian. By 1908, Fr. Valaitis and the St. George's Society were successful in establishing a Lithuanian church at Westminster and Cardoni

Coins made around 1928 for lunch at the Detroit Lithuanian Club, which was located a few blocks away from the Polish church, St. Josephat. Courtesy of Frank Passic.

avenues. Bishop Foley blessed the structure in 1909. When Fr. Valaitis left in 1915, his replacement, Fr. Casimir Skrypkus, took on the task of building a brick church at 1313 Westminster Street. The completed new church was blessed by Bishop Gallagher in 1917.

An energetic, intellectual priest, Fr. Fabian Kemėšis, replaced Fr. Skrypkus in 1919. Fr. Kemėšis was one of the most active priests in Lithuanian colonies during this time. He had been editor of the Lithuanian Chicago newspaper *Draugas* ("Friend") and the East Coast paper *Darbininkas* ("Worker"). He revived the Knights of Lithuania in Detroit and built the parish school in 1920. He left the parish two years later and ultimately returned to Lithuania and died in Siberia in 1954 during the Soviet regime.[32]

Under Fr. Kemėšis, the Lithuanian community experienced its first geographic division. These Lithuanians organized the St. Anthony's Society in 1910 and later the Knights of Lithuania, Lodge 79, and the Lithuanian Roman Catholic Alliance, Lodge 190. By the end of World War I, about 150 Lithuanian families were living and working on the west side of Detroit (west of Woodward Avenue). They worked at the new Ford, Cadillac, and Timken factories. Two Lithuanian communities lived on the West Side. The first and larger area was bordered by Michigan Avenue, Dix (Vernor) Highway, and 18th and 25th streets, with a section off of 25th. and Bagley streets going to Vinewood, known as *žiurkiakaimo* ("rats' village"). The second area was just east of Dearborn within an area bound by the Central, Springwell, and Lawndale streets, along Longworth Street. These West Side Lithuanians complained about the amount of time needed to get to St. George's Parish on the East Side, as a direct route did not exist. In 1919, the West Side community reorganized the St. Anthony's Society to benefit the west side Lithuanians. The new St. Anthony's Society president, Motiejus Bendoraitis, immediately sought a place on the West Side to worship in Lithuanian and organize Lithuanian cultural groups. In 1920 he found a Bohemian parish, St. John Nepomucene, on the corner of Ash and Lawton streets, which would allow for Lithuanian worship. Fr. Kemėšis came and later sent newly ordained Fr. Boreišis. The society saw Fr. Boreišis as the future pastor of a Lithuanian parish on the West Side. The St. Anthony's Society created a parish committee to search for a suitable place to break ground and to approach the Detroit bishop for permission. Despite reluctance, due to the small number of Lithuanians on the West Side, Bishop Gallagher allowed the parish to be created as St. Anthony's Lithuanian Parish. The site selected was on the corner of 25th Street and Vernor. In December of 1920, Bishop Gallagher announced that Fr. Boreišis would be the pastor of the parish. The parish held Mass at St. John Nepomucene until St. Anthony's Lithuanian Parish was built in 1923.[33]

A couple members of the committee resigned because their suggestion of building in the Lawndale Street area closer to the Ford factory was turned down. The next Lithuanian parish, St. Peter's, was created in this area on Longworth Street in 1920. This parish was always the smallest of the three, even after the third wave of immigrants arrived. It was closed down in 1995, as the Lithuanian population in the area dwindled and other ethnic groups took over.

In 1923, the pastors for St. Anthony's and St. George's had something in common. Both were seminarians and ordained priests from the Polish seminary in Orchard Lake Michigan, S.S. Cyril and Methodius. This seminary was opened in 1888 in Detroit on St. Aubin Street between Forest Avenue and Garfield Street. The first Lithuanian priest to attend the seminary was Fr. Valaitis, the founding priest of St. George's. This could not have happened without the help of one of the seminary's founders, Rev. Jozef Dabrowski, and his kindly disposition toward Lithuanians.[34] In 1893, after being deported out of Lithuania for having illegal literature, Antanas Kaupas joined the seminary in Detroit. He started the St. Casimir's Society of Science in the seminary, which was instrumental in bringing and keeping Lithuanian-Americans in the Polish seminary. He taught the Lithuanian language at the seminary until

Interior view of S.S. Peter and Paul Church, pre-1962. Courtesy of the Grand Rapids History and Special Collections, Archives, Grand Rapids Public Library, Grand Rapids, Michigan.

he became a priest in 1896. Fr. Kaupas was sent to a parish at Wilkes-Barre, Pennsylvania. After he left, the Polish professors began to persecute the Lithuanians for speaking Lithuanian. Fewer and fewer Lithuanians attended. The trend changed when the seminary was moved to Orchard Lake, about forty miles to the northwest of Detroit, in 1909. Between 1910 and 1920, twenty-five Lithuanians attended the seminary. Ignas Boreišis, P. Lapelis, and Augustas Petraitis were instrumental in reviving the St. Casimir's Society into the Lithuanian Students' St. Casimir's Society at the Polish Seminary (Lietuvių moksleivių Šv. Kazimiero Dragija Lenkų Seminarijoj) and the Lithuanian Hope Society (Lietuvių Viltis Draugija).[35] Beginning in 1920, Lithuania was at war with Poland and the Polish professors again persecuted Lithuanians for speaking their native language. Ultimately, Lithuanians stopped attending the seminary, but Lithuanian-Americans should be thankful for the impact this Polish seminary made on the Lithuanian-American community.

The Grand Rapids parish, S.S. Peter and Paul Church, started a little sooner than the Detroit parish of St. George. Much as in Detroit, the Lithuanians of Grand Rapids attended mass at the Polish parish, St. Adalbert's, at 5th and Davis streets. Lithuanians also attended the German St. Mary's

"Kitchen Crew," S.S. Peter and Paul Aid Society, 1948. Courtesy of the Grand Rapids History and Special Collections, Archives, Grand Rapids Public Library, Grand Rapids, Michigan.

parish at Turner and First streets. In 1891, Lithuanians began the S.S. Peter and Paul's Society at 399 Alpine Street.[36] Bishop Richter allowed a parish to be assembled for Lithuanians in 1902. Since no priest was available, Fr. Ponganis from St. Adalbert's drove in horse and buggy over to the S.S. Peter and Paul Society building to celebrate a Lithuanian Mass. Excavation for the new church began in 1903. Then Fr. Ponganis was transferred and all work stopped until Fr. Matulatis arrived as pastor. Fr. Matulaitis had been thrown out of Lithuania and finished his seminary work in the United States. He was moved all over the East and Midwest from Lithuanian parish to Lithuanian parish. The church and school were completed in 1907 under Fr. Matulaitis. The architecture of the building is unconventional because the church was on the second floor while the school was on the first.

Despite having a new church built, the community did not stabilize because the tenures of the priests were short. Between Fr. Matulaitis leaving in 1912 and Fr. Lipkus arriving in October of 1925, there were five pastors or administrators. A new church was also built under the direction of Fr.

Anthony Dexnis (Deksnis in Lithuanian; the Lithuanian alphabet does not have an "x") by 1924, which cost $96,000. This is the church building that still stands on Myrtle Street and Quarry Avenue.

Quite a few similarities exist between the parishes of Grand Rapids and Detroit. First, once the parish was established, the parish pastor stayed for quite a long time. Fr. Čižauskas stayed at St. George's for thirty-four years; Fr. Boreiša stayed at St. Anthony's for thirty-eight years; and, Fr. Lipkus stayed at S.S. Peter and Paul for thirty-six years. Whether these long tenures hurt the Lithuanian community could be debated. Did the long tenures stagnate the religious life of the Lithuanian community? As central as the parish seems to Lithuanian life, the verdict is mixed in connection to vocations. S.S. Peter and Paul Parish had a respectable number of clergy, with thirteen sisters and eight priests, one later becoming an archbishop of Oklahoma City. Detroit's St. Anthothy's had three priests and eleven sisters. St. George's (later assumed by Divine Providence) has had none.

The second similarity between the Lithuanian parishes of Michigan, and probably the more important of the two, is that the parish, as in Lithuania, became the center of Lithuanian cultural life. The parish became a place for Lithuanians to meet every week. Ideas were passed from one person to another and organizations began to grow from these ideas. As already seen, all the parishes grew from organizations within each of their respective Polish parishes.

Many of the organizations were created to help the parish, but at the same time they were intended to move the work of the church out into the community. This was a very important function for newly immigrated Lithuanians who did not have much with them. Many ethnic groups within American society created such organizations, which helped immigrants in time of need, death, or illness. Lithuanian immigrants did the same. These fraternal organizations in many cases were religious, but some were not. They also built meeting halls, where dances and meetings would take place. The meeting halls gave people another place to meet besides the parish on Sundays.

The oldest such group was the S.S. Peter and Paul Aid Society, founded in Grand Rapids in 1891. St. George's Society in Detroit began in 1903. Membership required a Roman Catholic affiliation. At the time, state insurance laws forbade the independent aid societies from functioning as insurance companies. The death payment was limited to $100. If an immigrant was a

Bishop Salatka of Marquette

The most prominent Lithuanian priest in the United States would have to be Archbishop Charles A. Salatka. Archbishop Salatka was born in Grand Rapids in 1918 and baptized at S.S. Peter and Paul Parish. His parents were married at that church in 1912. His father worked as a sander at a local furniture factory. Charles became an altar boy under Fr. Lipkus and soon began seminary studies at the age of fourteen at St. Joseph's Seminary in Grand Rapids. Finishing this program, he attended Catholic University of America, was ordained a priest in 1945, and continued his studies in Rome, earning two advanced degrees. Pope John XXIII elevated him to bishop and he was ordained in 1962 as titular bishop of Cariana and auxiliary bishop of Grand Rapids. In 1968 he was installed as ninth bishop of the Marquette Diocese. Bishop Salatka had to confront the closing of two-thirds of all the Catholic schools in the Upper Peninsula. He also started a program to support priests. In 1977 the Vatican appointed him archbishop of Oklahoma City. Archbishop Salatka retired in 1992 and died in 2003. Archbishop Charles A. Salatka is the only American of Lithuanian extraction to reach the level of bishop and later archbishop. The fact that he grew up in the Lithuanian neighborhood in Grand Rapids, Michigan, to immigrant parents should not be overlooked.

member of both societies, then he or she would get the benefits from two and get close to the amount needed.[37] These groups became successful and popular enough to ask for donations and build their own halls or expand and improve the old ones. These halls scheduled wedding receptions, political rallies, Lithuanian language classes, plays, operas, dances, concerts, and parties. A bar, where beer could be purchased, usually was built. Immigrants would make their rounds on weekends, going from one hall to another. One Lithuanian was quoted as saying, "I would go to church to cleanse my soul. But I went to my *svetainė* (hall) for a glass of beer and a good time."[38] In Grand Rapids, other societies formed, such as the Sons of Lithuania Aid Society and the Vytautas Aid Society. By World War II many of these groups were already holding their meetings in English.[39]

One of the better-known groups for women at this time was the Lithuanian American Roman Catholic Women's Alliance (LARCWA). This organization began in 1913 in New England and Pennsylvania and reached four

Lithuanian all women cast—Sons Hall, 1920s. Courtesy of the Grand Rapids History and Special Collections, Archives, Grand Rapids Public Library, Grand Rapids, Michigan.

hundred members nationwide by the time of its first convention in 1915. Grand Rapids began its organization in 1917 as Chapter 42. Grand Rapids hosted the national convention in 1945. This is one of the few organizations in Grand Rapids to have a national affiliation. Although the LARCWA still works in Grand Rapids, many of these societies merged and slowly became defunct by the 1980s as their membership grew old and died. New waves of Lithuanian immigrants generally did not join these organizations.

Detroit's St. George's Parish began its LARCWA Chapter 54 in 1919. St. Anthony started Chapter 64 in 1927 and Chapter 51 in 1947. Chapter 54's motto, "Work for the church, nation and humankind" (*"Dirbti bažnyčiai, tautai, ir žmonijai"*), sums up what all these support organizations did. They would financially and morally support the parish, cultural groups (like the women's choir in Chapter 54's case), and the parish school, and/or send packets to Lithuania. As with many of the first- and second-wave organizations, the membership within the chapters is dwindling nationally. Detroit Chapter 54 voted itself out of existence in 1994 at its 75th anniversary celebration.[40] First- and second-wave Detroit organizations, just like those in Grand Rapids, did not increase their membership with the new waves of immigrants and today are becoming defunct.

The largest and most popular of the organizations of the first and second waves in Detroit was The Knights of Lithuania, or Vyčiai (pronounced VEE-chay) in Lithuanian. This group was first organized in Lawrence, Massachusetts, on April 27, 1913, under the motto, "For God and Country." Members have to be Lithuanian to some extent or married to a Lithuanian. St. Casimir, the patron saint of Lithuania, is the organization's patron. The purpose of the organization was to unite Lithuanian youth living in the United States and preserve Lithuanian culture. Later the group worked toward the freedom of Lithuania, after it fell to the Soviets. Since the independence of Lithuania in 1991, the Knights send aid to the Lithuanian Pontifical College in Rome, ship medical supplies to Lithuania, supply Roman Catholic reading material to Lithuania, and have begun an "Adopt a Lithuanian Seminarian" program. Within the United States the Knights support Lithuanian culture through lectures, trips, and choral and dance groups. They have a Knights of Lithuania Foundation and a scholarship fund. The Knight's "Aid to Lithuania, Inc." has raised over $475,000 from members, exchanged the money for medicine and medical supplies, and shipped it to Lithuania.[41]

In Detroit, the Knights have been an active organization. St. Anthony's Parish started Local Council 102 under the active support of Fr. Kemėšis. Thirteen youth joined at the beginning. The group soon had 67 members with its own choir, baseball and basketball teams, and theatre group. During World War II, the council actively supported the political drive for the re-independence of Lithuania. They sent letters and packages to soldiers. By 1945 the chapter had 160 members. The chapter actively supported displaced persons (DP's) from Lithuania. As DP's became the third wave of Lithuanian immigrants, the Knights started a Lithuanian language school on Saturdays and helped start Camp Dainava. Some DP's joined, but not many. Council 102 is still an active council, according to the Knights of Lithuania web homepage. Divine Providence Parish in Southfield had a council, but not much is known about the council, Number 79.

Detroit has been an important city for the Knights of Lithuania. The councils, especially 102, have been active throughout the twentieth century. Detroit hosted the Knights' National Convention for the first time in 1922. Detroit went on to host the convention four more times, in 1948, 1959, 1974, and

1995. Compared to other cities, Detroit is tied for third with Cleveland and Dayton for this honor. Chicago has hosted the convention thirteen times and Boston six. The Knights have been the longest lasting and most active of the first- and second-wave immigrant organizations in Detroit. Unfortunately, it is becoming a smaller part of the community as members grow older and pass on, just as in Grand Rapids.

First- and second-wave Lithuanian immigrants across the United States created many other organizations, like the Lithuanian Roman Catholic Alliance of America, the Lithuanian Alliance of America, the Lithuanian Socialist Alliance, the Lithuanian Roman Catholic Federation of America, and the Lithuanian Nationalist "Sandara" Association. These organizations, like the fraternal organizations, helped immigrants with insurance, economic needs, American citizenship, and socialization, but these groups had a wider scope of activity as well. These organizations also pushed a political agenda. This agenda generally was to help Lithuania's government through financial donations set up through funds and to pressure American politicians, especially the executive branch, to help Lithuania's cause for independence.

Americans trying to understand these organizations from a political point of view may have a difficult time. American politics generally can be seen in light of two views: Democrat or Republican. Lithuanian politics has no easy one-to-one correlation to this two-party system. The politics of Lithuania had many influences the American system dealt with as anomalies. Lithuania was impacted by socialism, nationalism, and the Roman Catholic Church. Not surprisingly, the Lithuanian organizations created for political ends and means fell under these headings.

The oldest of these organizations, the Lithuanian Roman Catholic Alliance of America (LRKSA), was created in Plymouth, Pennsylvania, in 1886. The organization united the different Catholic organizations created in the larger Lithuanian colonies. Most of these organizations were on the Eastern seaboard, with a couple contributions from Chicago. The clerical nature of the LRKSA meant that not much room was made for socialist or nationalist views.

At first, the socialists and nationalists united in response to the LRKSA. They formed the Lithuanian Alliance of America (SLA) in Wilkes-Barre, Pennsylvania, in 1901 when they walked out of the LRKSA convention. The nationalists and socialists, called the freethinkers, found a new meeting location down the street and began their own convention. This organization has gone through ups and downs through the decades, but still had a membership of 8,001 in 1971, with over three million dollars in capital.[42]

Even though the Lithuanian Alliance has survived to the present, it also created splinter groups that went off to organize their own parties. In 1905, the Lithuanian Socialist Party of America organized itself, changing its name to the Lithuanian Socialist Alliance two years later. This organization went through many twists and turns as it tried to survive the swings in American socialism and a takeover by the Communist Party of America. The nationalists splintered off into the Lithuanian Nationalist Association of America in 1915 in Brooklyn, New York. In 1918, they made their paper, *Sandara,* an official organ that still exists today.[43] Ultimately, Lithuanian immigrant political organizations, with their constituent funds and newspapers, fell into three camps: Catholic, Socialist, or Nationalist. Catholics by far outnumbered the other two.

As for Michigan, these organizations were established well before a Lithuanian population in Michigan could support such groups. These organizations were initiated and splintered by the time Grand Rapids or Detroit was ready for such activity. As mentioned before, the Grand Rapids community did not join these large federal organizations, while the Detroit community did. Even Traverse City had a chapter in the LRKSA with two delegates, V. Deimanta and P. Mikolainis, at the convention in Wilkes-Barre in 1901.[44] A large political convention of 1,101 Lithuanian delegates was organized at New York's Madison Square Gardens on March 13, 1918, to find ways to promote Lithuania's independence, which the Lithuanian Council (Lietuvos Taryba) declared on February 16, 1918. This convention sent a resolution to President Wilson and to the Allied governments asking them to recognize Lithuania. Two-thirds of the delegates represented Roman Catholic organizations and one-third represented Nationalist interests. The Socialists decided not to join in this convention despite an invitation. Of all the states, Pennsylvania had the most delegates, with 258, while Michigan had 7.[45]

Detroit was important to the LRKSA to some extent. The 33rd convention of the LRKSA was held in Detroit in June 1918. "Only" 42 delegates showed up. The last time such low numbers attended was when the organization first moved its convention site off the eastern seaboard to Chicago in 1908. Delegates totaled 31 that year. By the 1936 convention of the LRKSA,

Michigan had seven chapters with a total of 349 members. This was good for the seventh-largest delegation per state.[46] The LRKSA experience shows the importance of Michigan to Lithuanian immigrants. Michigan did not have a large enough group of immigrants to have a large impact on Lithuanian émigré politics, but large enough to be counted.

The Soviet invasion and incorporation of Lithuania invigorated Lithuanian first- and second-wave political organizations. In Pittsburgh on August 9, 1940, the Lithuanian Catholic Federation of America met in response to the Soviet invasion of Lithuania in September 1939. The meeting called for the establishment of a Council for Aid to Lithuania. On May 15, 1941, this council was renamed the Lithuanian American Council (Amerikos Lietuvių Taryba, or ALTas). ALTas was opened to all Lithuanian groups that stood for a free and independent Lithuania and pledged to work toward this goal. Nationalists quickly joined and the invitation was extended to other groups. Before the name change, the council had already met with President Franklin Roosevelt, on October 15, 1940. The initial work by ALTas got the State Department to agree not to recognize the Soviet takeover of Lithuania. ALTas became instrumental in creating the United Lithuanian Relief Fund for helping Lithuanian refugees.[47] The organization also found family sponsors for displaced persons immigrating to the United States after World War II.

In terms of ALTas, Michigan played a role. Although most of the ALTas branches were headquartered on the East Coast, Detroit held the Seventh Congress of ALTas in 1969. The organizer of this congress was the Detroit area president, Kazys Veikutis. Despite the first- and second-wave predominance within this organization, the organizers for this congress included many third-wave Lithuanians. Although Detroit held this congress, only one Michigan Lithuanian, Elzbieta Pauražiene, sat on the council for this year. The council had twenty-nine members, mostly from the Chicago area. The congress did make itself noticeable to many American politicians. Five governors, nine U.S. senators, forty-four U.S. representatives, and Chicago Mayor Daley joined the congress as honorary members.[48]

On a more local level, the Detroit area ALTas organized community lectures on special occasions during the year to keep Lithuania's cause in the community's mind. These usually were held in the gym at Divine Providence church. A notable speaker from outside the Detroit area was invited to speak for an hour and then a cultural program took place with singing, poetry, or folk dancing. If possible, U.S. or state politicians would attend as honored guests. The meetings always started and ended with Lithuanian hymns or the Lithuanian national anthem. These meetings sponsored by ALTas continued into the 1990s.

After all this political activity in the United States, were Lithuanians of the first and second wave in Michigan politically oriented toward the Democrats or the Republicans? No major Lithuanian political figures arose in this time period in Michigan. No studies of Lithuanian views toward the American political system in Michigan were conducted at this time. Conjecture is the only tool available for an answer. Considering the sociological background of Lithuanians immigrating to Michigan between 1870 and 1940, one could only guess that they were left of center. As mentioned, Lithuanians were generally uneducated and unskilled workers. They lived in urban, industrial areas and had experience with socialist ideas. Their main focus was to improve their own economic situation and improve Lithuania's political situation. With all of this in mind and if conjecture had to be made, Lithuanians were probably more Democratic than Republican by 1940.

Anecdotal information from other areas of the country could also prove to be useful in this conjecture. If Lithuanians in other urban, industrial areas were more likely to be Democrat, then this could be true for urban, industrial Lithuanians in Michigan as well. Lithuanians played a role in strikes and unions in the east. Some were even shot during a strike in the Pennsylvania coal mining area of Lattimer in October 1897.[49] Pennsylvania Lithuanians became Democrats, according to historian David Fainhauz, although Lithuanian Republican organizations did meet in the Philadelphia area. But, according to him, Lithuanians elected in municipal elections were Democrat. *The Lithuanian World Directory of 1963* shows nine separate Lithuanian Democratic clubs and no Republican clubs in the Chicago area. The same directory has no Lithuanian Democratic or Republican clubs in Detroit (although a socialist club and a nationalist club were in place). Lithuanian Democrats had an easier time getting elected than did Republican Lithuanians in Chicago. These anecdotes point to the possibility that Michigan Lithuanians were likely Democrats.

Politically, Lithuanian immigrants in Michigan during the first and second waves joined Lithuanian organizations to help themselves through insurance and socialization programs and help the family back in Lithuania. Their association with these organizations reflects their political traditions from Lithuania, not from America. They joined mostly Catholic or Nationalist organizations to push Presidents Wilson, Harding, and Franklin Roosevelt to help Lithuania during times of crisis. Lithuanians donated money to funds organized by these associations and sent hundreds of thousands of dollars to Lithuania. Michigan Lithuanians played a role in these activities, but not a big one. In the end, these organizations lost membership and have the same problems that the aforementioned fraternal organizations are having today. Detroit seems to be the last colony in Michigan that keeps these vestigal organizations from the first and second waves intact.

Despite Detroit Lithuanians' more national outlook, the Detroit and Grand Rapids Lithuanian communities revealed some striking contrasts and comparisons during this time. They were both industrial cities that offered relatively easy employment for Lithuanian immigrants. Both communities began about the same time and created Catholic parishes, concentrated neighborhoods, and support and cultural organizations.

The striking difference is in their relationships to the larger Lithuanian community abroad. Grand Rapids largely left itself out of the larger Lithuanian organizations, like the Knights of Lithuania or the LRKSA. They had their own aid societies, like the Sons and Daughters of Lithuania Aid Society, and did not create chapters of national organizations, as the Detroit community did. While the Detroit community slowly suburbanized, the local chapters of the national organizations stayed intact. Suburbanization meant the end of the Lithuanian neighborhoods in Detroit, but not in Grand Rapids. The effects of suburbanization have been slower in Grand Rapids. Even today, a drive through Lithuanian Town in Grand Rapids results in views of Lithuanian businesses, the Lithuanian parish, and the cemetery. Lithuanians still live in the old neighborhood.

In a final contrast, the Detroit community became larger as the years passed and profited from a larger influx of immigrants from the later immigrant waves. Transportation changes, higher income, and suburbanization dispersed the Detroit Lithuanian community but conversely offered more cultural and organizational opportunities connected to the larger Lithuanian community centered at the parish level. Grand Rapids became a smaller Lithuanian community and has kept its neighborhood identity

"Kapusta Burger Crew," Lithuanian Sons and Daughters Society, 1945. Courtesy of the Grand Rapids History and Special Collections, Archives, Grand Rapids Public Library, Grand Rapids, Michigan.

with the help of the insular organizations that were formed by first- and second-wave immigrants.

Unlike most first- and second-wave Lithuanian immigrant communities, which began in the urban and industrial areas of Michigan, the Lithuanian immigrant community in Mason and Lake counties began in a rural area. Lithuanian immigrants longing to return to the farm created this community. The community had its beginning in 1905 with the name Naujoji Lietuva (New Lithuania). New Lithuania was a business endeavor created by Anton Kiedis, a Lithuanian real estate developer of Scottville, Michigan. He worked from the People's State Bank Building in Scottville. He published a promotional booklet promising a farmer's paradise. Lithuanians were sent direct mailings promoting the real estate in eastern Mason and western Lake counties. The villages in this area are Scottville, Irons, Custer, Bachelor, Fountain, Peacock, and Free Soil. The booklet, published in the teens, claims that 360 Lithuanian farms had been established.[50] Farming was not as good as promised. Some areas did not grow much but cucumbers. But one became very successful. The Andrulis Dairy farm near Fountain has existed since 1919. The family business has passed through three generations of Andrulises and expanded

Old Country Farmer's Cheese

One business in Michigan that holds a Lithuanian name is Andrulis, also known as Michigan Farm Cheese Dairy. This factory produces over a million dollars worth of farmer's cheese from an old Lithuanian recipe. The Andrulis's factory is found near Fountain, Michigan, in Mason County in the area of Kiedis's New Lithuania. The Andrulis family has owned the business since it began in 1942 with Angelė and Jonas Andrulis. Both were born in the United States, to Lithuanian immigrants living in Chicago and Indiana. Angelė and Jonas started the business by making cheese from excess milk off their farm. The business grew as they marketed the cheese to Chicago, Wisconsin, and Detroit. They employed Lithuanians. They sold the business in 1962 to their son Allen, who increased the market by getting the product certified as kosher. Now Allen's daughter, Shannon, and her husband, Dan Thomas, manage the business. The business is now marketed to their traditional Midwest areas, but also to the large Jewish community in New York City. They also have a deal in the works for a joint venture to produce and sell the cheese in Lithuania.

its market to the East Coast.[51] Enough Lithuanians migrated to this area from Michigan cities, Chicago, the East Coast, and Lithuania to start a parish. St. Mary's Parish was established between Fountain and Custer in 1933. In 1958, the parish still had a Lithuanian pastor with some 150 Lithuanians attending.[52] The parish still exists today, but the pastor is not Lithuanian and there are no Lithuanian-language Masses. Most immigrants stayed on and died in Mason and Lake counties, as attested to by the area cemetery records.[53] Some Lithuanian families still live in the area.

Another out-state Lithuanian community established in the early 1900s was in the city of Albion. Albion is approximately sixteen miles west of Jackson along Interstate 94. Lithuanians in Albion went through the same experiences as Lithuanians in the larger cities, as attested to by Frank Passic. Passic, the town historian and of Lithuanian descent, has done a wonderful job of recording Lithuanian families in Albion for genealogical purposes.

Lithuanians arrived in Albion as early as 1901. Some Lithuanians were recruited straight from Lithuania to work at the Albion Malleable Iron Company. Others arrived by word of mouth from Cicero or Chicago, Illinois, or

*Mike Kulikowski (1890–1975) displays his 13-inch perch which won the 1955 fishing con-
test at the Albion Malleable Iron Company. Mike was born in Lithuania, immigrated
to Chicago and moved to Albion, Michigan in 1918 to work at the company. Courtesy
of Frank Passic.*

from other parts of Michigan. Employment in the factories or the coal mine
brought these Lithuanians to Albion. The factories mostly fabricated auto-
mobile parts. The low-grade coal mines opened for a short time during the
coal shortages of World War I, then closed. One was owned by a Lithuanian,
John Shimkus, and kept open until 1940.

Another Lithuanian business owner was Albert Jasenas. As a young man,
Albert worked in the Civilian Conservation Corps in a group that worked on
the Isle Royale. In Albion he operated a roller skating rink from 1939 to 1965
on the second floor of a hardware store. He then became the plant manager
of the Johnson Manufacturing Company in Albion. Tragically, Albert was
stabbed to death in his home in Albion in 1984.

After World War II, more Lithuanians went to work in Albion factories.
Lithuanians are recognized on a historical marker at the Riverside Cemetery,

where many are buried. Lithuanians still live in Albion and are recognized during Albion's annual "Festival of the Forks." The recognition of Lithuanians at the festival did not come until relatively recent times—1978, to be exact. Frank Passic still operates a booth at the festival and a Lithuanian flag is flown along with flags of other ethnicities of Albion on Superior (Main) Street during the week of the festival.[54]

The Upper Peninsula was also home to Lithuanian immigrants. They worked as copper miners, lumberjacks, or farmers, and a few owned stores. The 1930 Census shows Lithuanians living in every county of the Upper Peninsula except for Baraga County. According to the 1930 Census, Lithuanians coming to the Upper Peninsula migrated from Chicago or Wisconsin, since many of these immigrants' children are documented as being born in Illinois or Wisconsin. A few Lithuanians living in Mackinac County as loggers were documented as being 100 percent Lithuanian but were born in Illinois and Indiana. The distribution of Lithuanians across the Upper Peninsula also shows that they came from Wisconsin. The highest concentrations of Lithuanians in the Upper Peninsula are nearest the Wisconsin border. Fewer and fewer Lithuanians are found living in the eastern counties.

Many of the Lithuanians living near the Wisconsin border worked as farmers in Menominee County. Today the county is still considered "the dairy capital of the Upper Peninsula." The county has a productive soil, unlike the rest of the forested, rocky, or sandy Upper Peninsula. The agrarian immigrant Lithuanian families owned farms in Cedarville, Daggett, and Nadeau in Menominee County. A Lithuanian farm was also found in Schoolcraft County and another in Mackinac County.

A large employer of Lithuanian immigrants in the Upper Peninsula was mining. Lithuanian iron miners are found in Marquette, Dickinson, Iron, and Gogebic counties. These last three counties border Wisconsin. In Houghton and Keweenaw counties they mined copper. The largest concentration of Lithuanians was in the Painesdale area in the Copper Country. The Painesdale area encompasses Painesdale, Baltic, and South Range. Along with other Catholic immigrants, the Lithuanians helped establish Holy Family Parish in South Range in 1914. The priests were mostly of Eastern European descent. The name of the second pastor, who served from 1915 to 1918, Fr. Stanislaus Jaksztys, sounds Lithuanian.[55] The Lithuanians in the area did have a benevolent society named the Sons of Lithuania, which began in

Lithuanian Jews

A close study of names in the Federal census records shows that there was a small Jewish Lithuanian community in Detroit in 1910. However there were immigrants located in Michigan's smaller towns as well. Some of these Lithuanians came to United States in the 1860s and migrated to Michigan soon after. They worked in a variety of occupations in Detroit where several dozen families were centered. Although Grand Rapids became home to a large Lithuanian community there were no Jews there in 1910.

1910.[56] The 1920 Census showed 149 entries for Lithuanian immigrants, while the 1930 Census had 42. As copper mining declined, which happened around this period, Lithuanians must have left for employment elsewhere. Today, not much is left of the Lithuanian community in Painesdale. Holy Family Parish was closed in the 1980s during a cycle of diocesan streamlining. The local telephone book still carries a few Lithuanian surnames from the 1930 Census in the Painesdale area.

Logging was a huge industry in Michigan, but by 1930 it was on its third decade of decline. Logging would have been an easy job to get for a Lithuanian, since it did not require any education. Not much information is available about Lithuanian loggers, save for the U.S. Census. The 1930 Census shows that Lithuanian immigrants documented as loggers were single and living in logging camps in the wilderness counties of Michigan far from Lithuanian colonies or were boarders in logging towns. These immigrants moved from place to place as their worksite shifted with the supply of lumber. Lithuanian loggers lived in all Upper Peninsula counties except for Baraga. Lithuanian loggers were the only Lithuanians living in Alger and Chippewa counties in 1930.

Lithuanian Jews also immigrated with the first wave. The 1930 Census documents quite a few Jews whose entries show a birthplace as Lithuania, but the language spoken at home is Yiddish, Jewish, or Hebrew. Lithuanian Jews tended to take on commercial business. Louis Getz opened a dry goods store in Marquette, as did Samuel Lowenstein in Ishpeming. Abraham and Joseph Fines were grocery store proprietors in Marquette. In Wayne County, Max Shapiro sold jewelry in Detroit and Abe Weiss was a real estate agent.

Getz Store, 1910. Courtesy of the Marquette County Historical Society.

Louis Getz

Louis Getz (1848–1935) was attracted to the economic possibilities in Michigan's rather isolated Upper Peninsula. Getz was born in Lithuania, then a part of Russia, in 1848 and emigrated to the United States in 1867. Four years later he went to the Lake Superior country where he worked as a traveling salesman in Houghton and Ontonagon counties. He settled in Michigamme, where he opened his first dry goods business and later formed a partnership with Maurice Paradise. Recognizing the importance of the city of Marquette, Getz moved his dry goods store there in 1886 where he became the sole proprietor. The business was a success and soon had to move into expanded quarters, where it has remained ever since, that have been known as Getz Department Store since 1910. Today the store is a Marquette landmark, still operated by family members, and home to a thriving business in Carhartt clothing both in shop and on-line.

According to the 1930 Census, Lithuanian Jewish immigrants also ran and owned hotels, pool halls, clothing stores, and restaurants.

In contrast, very few Lithuanian immigrants owned a business. Marenisco in the Upper Peninsula's Gogebic County had a Lithuanian restaurant owner by the name of Charles Perle. In Adams Township in Houghton County (this would be the Painesdale area) an Andrew Mickus managed a general store and a John McMeis (the 1930 Census documents him as Lithuanian, although the name is of Scottish origin) operated a pool room. The Upper Peninsula is a microcosm of Lithuanian immigrants in Michigan. Although they worked in unskilled labor positions like miner, farmer and logger, Lithuanians also held jobs as truck drivers, blacksmiths, cooks, chemical plant workers, and county park gardeners. In Henry Ford's factory in Kingsford, a Lithuanian was a machinist. Lithuanians worked in many jobs across all of Michigan, but rarely did they own a business.

Lithuanians and Sports

The first wave of Lithuanians coming to Michigan in the late 1800s did not have a concept of sports. In their cultural history, Lithuanians did not have sports as we know them today. No wonder the first wave of Lithuanian immigrants did not organize sports teams or worry about sports prowess. Survival on the farm in the old country and survival in the city in the new world was much more important.

Sports did matter to the second-generation Lithuanians and to the next two waves of immigrants. The 1920s and 1930s saw the first Lithuanian-American sports stars like Jack Sharkey (Juozas Zukauskas), heavyweight boxing champion of the world. This time period also saw the organization of the first Lithuanian sports teams. Detroit and Grand Rapids had a rivalry in baseball and basketball. In Grand Rapids, the S.S. Peter and Paul parish established the Lithuanian Athletic Club (LAC) in the fall of 1927. They invited the St. George's Parish of Detroit Athletic Club to compete in basketball in Grand Rapids in the winter of that year. Grand Rapids won the first competition. Subsequent games in Detroit were losses for Grand Rapids.[57]

Besides their place as a forum for inter-immigrant competition, these sports were also ways to compete in the hometown. The Grand Rapids LAC sported basketball, baseball, and football teams that competed in local leagues or with local teams if no league existed. Unfortunately, these teams did not survive after World War Two. In the last two decades, the Detroit Lithuanian community has had basketball and softball teams competing in city leagues. The Detroit club is well and thriving.

In Detroit the Lithuanian sports club is named Kovas (The Fight), and it was founded in the late 1940s and early 1950s. Since then, many cities with sizable Lithuanian immigrant communities have formed sports clubs to practice and then compete in annual tournaments between city clubs in a range of sports. Basketball is the most popular sport among the Lithuanian communities. Other sports they compete in, depending on the interest and time of year, include volleyball, track, tennis, golf, hockey, sharp shooting, swimming, table tennis, and chess. The membership of Kovas has waxed and waned over the years. The tournaments are rotated from city to city and managed by the host city's club, usually in April or over Memorial Day weekend. Tournaments have been held in the United States in Chicago, Detroit, New York, Boston, and Cleveland; in Canada in Toronto and Hamilton; and in Lithuania, since its independence in 1991.

Detroit has a physical distinction that the other Lithuanian communities in Michigan or other states do not have: the Lithuanian Cultural Center has a social area, a gymnasium with a full-length basketball court, and the Divine Providence Parish connected to it. Therefore, a basketball and/or volleyball game can take place before a dance as entertainment on Friday night. Refreshments can be served while a game is commencing. On Saturday the tournaments are run at local high schools and/or at the Schoolcraft Community College. Then on Sunday, competitors can attend mass at Divine Providence Parish, walk down the hall to the gym, and eat lunch while watching one of the finals in the gym. The passage from the spiritual/religious event to the cultural event gives tournaments in Detroit a seamlessness that other Lithuanian communities in North America cannot match.[58]

Darius Steponas, a first-wave immigrant, imported basketball and baseball to Lithuania during the independent inter-war years. Baseball did not become popular, but basketball became the national sport in Lithuania. With the help of Lithuanian-Americans on their team, the Lithuanian basketball team won the European Championship in 1937 and 1939. The popularity of the sport exploded among Lithuanian youth, both men and women. Today, Lithuania, a country with less than four million citizens, is a magnet for division I college basketball scouts. The University of Hawaii

Detroit Kovas Boys' Class D champions of the first Lithuanian World Sports Games held at Toronto, Canada in 1978.

had four Lithuanians on their team in 2001. Since 1990, names like Arvydas Sabonis, playing for the Portland Trailblazers, and Šarūnas Ilgauskas, playing for the Cleveland Cavaliers, are well known among NBA fans. In 2003, the Sacramento Kings drafted Darius Songaila, a Wake Forest University star.

Detroit's Kovas has supported both men's and women's basketball teams for many different age groups and abilities. The men's A team always includes former college players and the boys' A team recruits many high school players that will play in college. The youngest age group for basketball has usually been the eight- to ten-year-olds, labeled the D League. At the first World Lithuanian Games in Toronto, Canada, in 1978 (organized under the leadership of future Lithuanian president, Valdas Adamkus), the Detroit D team won the gold medal. This team included four future NCAA Division I players and a future University of Michigan football player. This team later played at the Boys' A League tournament in the World Lithuanian Games in Chicago in 1983 with the same D team, but older, with an addition of two more future NCAA Division I players. They won the gold in the finals against an Australian-Lithuanian All-Star team. Many of this same team also qualified to play in the boys' B team and won the gold medal in that age group in the finals against New York LAK (Lietuvių Atletų Klubas). Detroit Kovas was at its height at the World Lithuanian Games of 1983, not only because it medaled in

Detroit Kovas Men's Class B champions of the North American Lithuanian Sports Festival held on Long Island, New York in 1987.

many of the age groups in basketball, but also because it won the All Games Trophy for medaling more than any other club in all sports.

Through the years the membership of the club has gone up and down. The boys' D age group usually is the first to suffer a lack in membership and in the late 1980s and early 1990s the C age group was lacking. These age groups, in some years, did not compete in a tournament because many cities lacked members of that age. Women's teams also become a casualty. Some years there are women's basketball and volleyball teams, some years just volleyball, sometimes neither. Since the independence of Lithuania in 1991, opening the doors for more immigration to the United States, the membership of sports clubs like Kovas has exploded. In some cases, cities have created new sports clubs and new age divisions. The new clubs tend to include only fifth-wave immigrants. Today clubs have added two new age divisions: *molekuliu* (molecules) for five- to eight-year-olds, and the thirty-five and older group.

Golf and bowling were other sports in which Lithuanians successfully competed. Second-generation Lithuanians became interested in these sports initially because of their moneymaking prospects. Teenagers could supplement the family income by caddying at local country clubs or pin setting at the local bowling alley. Archbishop Salatka, as a youngster, caddied at a Grand Rapids country club during the Great Depression. On slow days the boss or owner would sometimes allow free games and practice. Practice led to Lithuanians becoming known in their area for these sports. Vic and Ed Shapaila, brothers from Grand Rapids, became golf pros in California and Grand Rapids, respectively. Bob Sakocius dominated the amateur golf scene in West Michigan in the 1980s and 1990s by winning five West Michigan Amateur Golf Tournament titles.

In bowling, Vic Szeiva is the most well known Lithuanian. He set pins as a fifteen-year-old and later became a member of the 1939–40 state championship bowling team (sponsored by West Side Beer Distributing Company, owned by Felix Zukaitis, a Lithuanian), made up of Lithuanians from Grand Rapids. Later still, he competed in thirty-one national ABC tournaments, despite having a severe limp from childhood polio.[59]

Lithuanians in the United States are proud to say that linebacker Dick Butkus from Illinois and quarterback Johnny Unitas from Pennsylvania were professional football players with a Lithuanian heritage. Wide receiver Joe Jurevicius, from Pennsylvania, played for the 2003 Super Bowl Champion Tampa Bay Buccaneers. Football as a club sport among Lithuanians never became popular, although the Grand Rapids Lithuanians did organize a team for a short time. This team scrimmaged with other teams from the area.

Lithuanians love their sports and love cheering for their sports teams, whether it's Kovas, the University of Michigan Wolverines, the Michigan State Spartans, or one of the professional sports teams from Detroit. Despite lacking a sports heritage, first- and second-wave Lithuanian immigrants quickly acculturated into American sports.

The Third and Fourth Waves of Lithuanian Immigration to Michigan

The third wave of Lithuanian immigration came immediately after the upheaval of World War II. This new wave of Lithuanians had no way to reach the United States while the destroying armies of the Allies and Axis crisscrossed Europe. Between the Displaced Persons Act of 1948 and the Refugee Act of 1953, 30,300 Lithuanians immigrated to the United States.[60] Three thousand of those came to the Detroit area. The displaced persons (DP's, or *dipukai* in Lithuanian) were worlds apart from the first- and second-wave Lithuanians. This was because the third wave of Lithuanian immigration was a forced political exile of the educated and religious people. They would have been deported to Siberia (or worse), had they stayed in their home country, due to the Stalinist occupation of Lithuania. As immigrants in the free world, they took the lesson of Čičinskas much more to heart than had the first and second waves.

As the German Nazi Army retreated from Lithuania in July 1943, many Lithuanians (57,495 according to displaced persons records in the French, British, and American zones) left Lithuania with the German Army.[61] These Lithuanians left because they knew the political agenda of the Soviet government from the first occupation of Lithuania in 1940–41. Many intellectuals, religious, and non-communist politically affiliated Lithuanians were deported to Siberia because they could possibly mount a resistance against the

Stalinist Communist regime. When the Soviets returned in 1944, many from those same groups of people deported in 1940 did not want to stay, although many did stay to fight a guerilla war until the mid-1950s. The Lithuanians in the third wave of immigration left Lithuania for purely political reasons. They knew the Soviets would liquidate them for their beliefs. Essentially, the immigrants of the third wave were political exiles. By contrast, those of the first and second waves were primarily economic immigrants.

The first and second waves were also uneducated farmhands. They came to the United States and worked in the unskilled industrial jobs. By contrast, the third wave of Lithuanian immigrants was educated and literate. Lithuania's independence allowed for Lithuanian to be taught again, and an explosion of learning took place. Under the tsar's rule in 1913 there were 875 primary schools with 51,221 students. By 1940, with the end of independence, Lithuania had 2,743 primary schools with 341,299 students.[62] Independence did a lot for educating the Lithuanian. The intelligentsia over-represented the third-wave refugees because of their probability of being persecuted for their prominence in Lithuanian society. The contrast in education played a part in the problems that occurred between first- and second-wave immigrants and third-wave immigrants.

Their reasons for leaving Lithuania shaped who the immigrants were and what they would do when they reached some kind of settlement. The overriding goal was a return to the homeland (remember the story of Čičinskas at the beginning of the book). The third-wave immigrants never intended to stay in the West, but to return to an independent, democratic Lithuania. After a few years in the displaced persons camps in West Germany, the DP's saw the reality of long-term exile, but the idea of returning to Lithuania still permeated all of the third-wave organizations.[63] Politics became the driving force of the third-wave immigrants. They joined or created cultural groups, but even these organizations had the undertone of the politics of return. The idea was inescapable.

The Lithuanian community across the United States, including that in Michigan, held a siege mentality about culture. Culture had to be preserved. Assimilation was an enemy to be sandbagged whenever possible.[64] The Lithuanian culture that was maintained was the Lithuanian culture as the DP's remembered it in the 1930s: agricultural and religious. This later would cause an "identity crisis" among the children of DP's, once Lithuania became independent from the Soviet Union.

Campers at Heritage Camp at Camp Dainava do an activity on top of Cross Hill. The crosses were created by Lithuanian immigrants. Courtesy of Juozas Vaiciunas.

This siege mentality began in the DP camps in West Germany. Schools and universities were organized to keep Lithuanian education alive. The same youth organizations in Lithuania, like the Scouts and Ateitininkai (the Futurists), were reorganized. When third-wave immigrants reached the shores of the United States, the siege mentality was continued through these youth organizations, but also through Lithuanian Saturday schools and summer camps. Lithuanian culture had to be infused during the work week and on vacation.

The creation of youth camps in Michigan by the DP's had a major impact on Lithuanians in the United States and Canada. The impact comes from the proximity of these camps to the major Lithuanian colonies in Michigan and the Midwest. For instance, Camp Dainava in Manchester, about eighteen miles west-southwest of Ann Arbor, right on the Washtenaw-Jackson County line, is a four-hour drive from Chicago, a one-hour drive from Detroit, a four-hour drive from Cleveland, and a five-hour drive from Toronto. Camp Dainava was essentially the geographic center of four major Lithuanian communities.

The physical geography of Michigan also has much to do with the camp placement. Many Lithuanians come to Camp Dainava, Camp Pilėnai (right across the road from Camp Dainava), or Camp Rakas (near Custer in "New Lithuania") and exclaim how closely the forests, rolling hills, and small inland lakes remind them of Lithuania.[65] The weather is close to Lithuania's also, because of the mild affect of the Baltic Sea in Lithuania and the Great Lakes around Michigan. It's not a surprise, then, that they would choose a place like Michigan in which to live or to create a camp like Dainava. The geography of these places resembles Lithuania enough to give dipukai a feeling of physical return to Lithuania for a few weeks of the year in the summer or a few days in the winter.

Camp Dainava was created as a linguistic preserve; the brainchild of an ambitious Lithuanian chemical engineer and Catholic leader, Dr. Adolfas Damušis. In Nazi Germany, Dr. Damušis was charged with treason for his participation as vice-president of the Supreme Committee for the Liberation of Lithuania. He was put in Stutthof concentration camp and his execution was scheduled when Allied forces liberated him. He came to the United States in 1947 under special provisions for concentration camp inmates. By 1949, Dr. Damušis had become the president of a first-wave organization, the Lithuanian Roman Catholic Federation of America (LRCFA). At the organization's national congresses in 1950, 1952 (in Detroit), and 1954, he introduced resolutions to create a youth camp for Lithuanians in order to preserve the culture and language. His dream was within reach when he became the national chairman of LRCFA. He began fundraising and searching for a suitable location for the camp. After a search of about thirty different locations, in 1955 a farm near Manchester, Michigan, was found for sale by the University of Michigan. The farm was 226 acres in size, with a 10-acre lake centered within. An agreement was made for a $20,000 price tag.[66] Unfortunately, the LRCFA national board voted the idea down at the fall meeting of 1955. Dr. Damušis proceeded to create an autonomous branch of LRCFA, the Lithuanian American Roman Catholic Youth Camps, Inc. This was a nonprofit organization. Support grew for this organization so that the $6,000 down payment became available by the end of 1955. This "heist" of a first-wave organization for a DP agenda began the cleavage between the first and second waves and the new third wave.

The next hurdle in the creation of the camp was an old one: to keep the deed in the name of the Lithuanian laity and not the local bishop. This required going to the auxiliary bishop of Detroit for permission to deed the land to the organization and not to the bishop. Luckily, Bishop Zaleski's mother was Lithuanian.[67] Permission was given as long as the camp was not used for permanent housing of a religious order or a church. On December 7, 1955, Dr. Damušis, his wife Jadvyga, and Fr. Antanas Juška signed the deed in Manchester. The Lithuanian American Roman Catholic Federation Dainava, a lay organization, owned the land.[68]

Youth Camp Dainava (meaning "land of the songs") has operated since 1957 as a Lithuanian cultural oasis, mostly for the Ateitis members. Between 1957 and 1964, the donations of Lithuanian Americans allowed for capital improvements to be made. Electrical lines were run to the buildings in 1957. An asphalted road made travel all year round possible. An asphalted sports court was created for basketball, tennis, and volleyball. Eighteen thousand pine trees were planted as a forest between 1961 and 1965. (A tornado ripped through some of it in the mid-1980s.) All the buildings were made of cinder blocks with volunteer help from Lithuanian craftsmen like Mykolas Abarius. The buildings that stood in 1958 were insured at the value of $80,000.[69] Today a garage, a cafeteria with an eating hall, two barracks, a store and pavilion, a small home, and a heated two-story living quarters all sit on the land. These were all built by 1965. In 1987, the value of the camp was held at about $200,000. From 1956 to 1980, $200,043.29 had been donated to the camp.[70] Detroit Lithuanians led most of this work, with the help of Cleveland and Chicago Lithuanians. Detroit Lithuanians held most of the executive committee positions until the early 1990s, when more Chicago and Cleveland supporters took over.

Since the first camp in July of 1957, Camp Dainava has not had one year where there was not a group of Lithuanian boys and girls running, playing, singing, swimming, and folk dancing. The first official camp was held from July 14–27, 1957, for sixty-eight Lithuanian girls. The camp organizers were the Sisters of the Immaculate Conception of Mary (from Putnam, Connecticut), exiled from Lithuania. These nuns lived on the grounds and organized the camps during the summers until the 1970s. The first summer had about three hundred campers in five different organized camps, while the following year had over six hundred campers in six different organized camps.[71]

Soon, camps were not just for summer. The heated two-story building was built and dedicated to Dr. Adolfas Damušis in 1965. The Ateitis organization's high school branch rented the camp during Columbus Day weekend,

A counselor of Heritage Camp at Camp Dainava plays guitar in front of a traditional Lithuanian sculpture of Jesus named "Rupintojelis" or "Concerned Jesus." Courtesy of Juozas Vaiciunas.

Thanksgiving Day weekend, and the week between Christmas Day and New Year's Day. Lithuanians mostly drove or rode the train from Chicago, Detroit, Toronto, and Cleveland, but campers did fly in from New York, Seattle, Los Angeles, and Washington, D.C. While American youth relaxed at home during these school vacation days, the children of Lithuanian DP's listened to and gave lectures about Lithuanian history, culture, organization, and philosophy. These lecture weekends were the creation of Fr. Stasys Yla.[72] Later the college students' branch held a weeklong camp in January and a "super weekend" in February during the 1990s.

Today, organizations, Lithuanian or not, Roman Catholic or not, can rent the camp year-round. This is partly due to a family, working as camp managers, living on the grounds year-round. The family has lived on the campsite since the mid-1980s, when the nuns' house was converted into a heated housing unit. The camp manager has allowed for twenty-four-hour service to be available to the camping organization. The camp manager does not organize the activities, but makes sure all the physical services run smoothly. The live-in manager for most years has been non-Lithuanian, strangely enough. From 1991 to 1994 the son of a DP managed the camp and then for the next four years a fifth-wave Lithuanian immigrant managed the camp. The executive council cannot seem to find a suitable fit with a Lithuanian to take the managing position, however, which seems antithetical to the whole idea of the camp.

Over the years, many groups besides Ateitis organizations have used the facilities. The summer is always booked with Lithuanian organizations. Lithuanian Scouts use it for a week. The Ateitis youth and high school branches use it for two weeks apiece. The college branch no longer holds their weeklong camp. The family/adults branch uses a week's time. Other groups use the camp for a week during the summer. They include the Lithuanian (Saturday School) Teachers' Association, the Lithuanian Folk Dancing Teachers' organization Frontininkai (the Lithuanian Front), and the Lithuanian Heritage Camp, which is the only outing sponsored by Camp Dainava itself.

Heritage Camp is an interesting anomaly within the cultural oasis idea. The mission of the camp is to raise appreciation of the Lithuanian culture among the families that have fallen away from the Lithuanian colonies yet who have some (first- or second-wave) Lithuanian blood in them. In any case, most of the children attending this camp do not know the Lithuanian language and probably never will. Heritage Camp began in 1960 as the idea of Jadvyga Damušienė. At that time, it was organized by the Knights of Lithuania from Detroit. It disappeared in 1965 but reappeared in 1978 under the direct leadership of Mrs. Damušienė. The camp was organized by her and counseled by the children of the DP's. Third-wave immigrants and their children at this time tagged the camp with a semi-derogatory term, *Angliukų*, meaning "those of an English speaking background." By the 1990s, the Damušis family had returned to Lithuania, leaving the organization of the camp to the DP children. As the third-wave counselors became older, they took over the teaching positions. Campers, who have been going to Heritage Camp since they were young, have now taken the counseling positions. The leadership of the camp is slowly moving toward those who are not the children of the third wave. (Is this a portent of how Dainava will be run in the future?) Today Heritage Camp is one of the best-attended camps of the summer. In 2003, the camp had a population of 157, with 119 being paying campers. Interestingly, as the history of the Lithuanians in Michigan has shown, the largest state contingent within the camp was represented by Illinois, with 85. Michigan was second with 41.[73]

Non-Lithuanian organizations also rent the camp facilities, outside of the Lithuanian part of the calendar. A French Teachers' Association meets at Dainava occasionally. Saline Public Schools rent the facilities for their fifth grade science camps, which run through the month of May. During the winter, many Roman Catholic parishes from around Michigan rent the place for their Lenten youth retreats.

Generally speaking, Camp Dainava was built by third-wave Lithuanians for third-wave Lithuanian use. Third-wave use was further narrowed down to those who belonged to the Roman Catholic organization Ateitis. Camp Dainava is amazing in its ability to thrive with such a narrowly defined population within the American population. The camp could not have been a success without its utility to the Lithuanians of the third wave. The importance and success of Camp Dainava lies in its central location among the large Lithuanian colonies of the Midwest. Camp Dainava allowed for the children of DP Lithuanians to meet, discuss, and remember the Lithuanian culture. Beyond this, Camp Dainava created an annual routine among Lithuanian organizations to meet and discuss short- and long-term goals. Dainava became instrumental in giving Lithuanian organizations a problem solving frame of mind. During the summer, many of the Lithuanian organizations would hold their annual organizational meetings where delegates would vote on resolutions. Dainava made this convenient.

Another form of cultural oasis idea was the formation of Lithuanian Saturday schools. Lithuanian Saturday school was a weekly oasis during the school year. Forms of this school existed in the first and second waves, but the third immigration wave made Saturday school an institution. The children of immigrant children from pre-school age to the twelfth grade would meet for an immersion in the Lithuanian language and culture. All subjects were taught in Lithuanian throughout the five-hour school day. Emphasis was on reading, writing, and grammar courses, but Lithuanian geography, history, religion, chorus, and folk dancing each had their periods. Each class had a different teacher, and grammar, writing, literature, history and religion each had a textbook. Grade reports were given to parents two to three times a year for each subject. The curriculum changed as the resource pool changed. At first the curriculum was created with what teachers had handily available: books brought from Lithuania or Germany. A Canadian printing press created Lithuanian workbooks and textbooks in the late 1950s. Saturday schools became organized nationwide under the Education Committee within the overarching organization called the Lithuanian Community (Lietuvių Bendruomenė, or LB). By 1967 a curriculum from kindergarten to twelfth grade was established.

Obviously, the school was important for the whole Lithuanian community. Plays and performances were attended by the community in general and reinforced the cultural values of the community. The school performed an annual play for the Christmas program called *Kalėdos Eglutė*, or The Christmas Tree. Many years the play required sets, extra rehearsals, and a choir. The school choir and the school's folk dance group performed for the February 16th (1918) Independence Day Celebration (*minėjimas*). The graduation of eighth graders to high school (most did not go on in their Lithuanian education after eighth grade) and twelfth graders was a community celebration with the choir singing and the folk group dancing. The school choir sang in the Lithuanian Song Festivals and the school folk dancing group performed in the Lithuanian Folk Dance Festival every four years. Saturday school was more than education, but a reinforcement of the culture and values of third-wave Lithuanian immigrants and their memories of an independent Lithuania and an ultimate return to one.

Michigan has had at least four different Saturday schools and a fifth is about to be created in Union Pier. At one time, Detroit had three Saturday schools and Grand Rapids one. Saturday schools were a spontaneous creation. Parents in major Lithuanian centers created these schools after seeing the poor quality of the Lithuanian taught at the Lithuanian parish schools.[74] The first- and second-wave Lithuanians in Detroit did send their children to the parish schools at St. George's and St. Anthony's but by the time the third wave came in the late 1940s, very little if any Lithuanian was taught during the school day. Third-wave parents began a school in Detroit in October 1949 with the help of St. Anthony's pastor, Fr. Boreišis. He allowed the classes to be conducted at the parish school on Saturdays with no rental fee. Parents taught the classes themselves and used what resources they had brought with them from Germany. The primary school began with thirty students and grew during the year, but little else is known, since little or no documentation has survived.

The Detroit community started a Lithuanian Teachers' Association in 1950, which became the administrative and financial support group for the school in Detroit. Out of lack of time and energy, the association folded in 1954, but not before it found a replacement. The LB Detroit Area Board took over the administration of the school in September 1954. In March 1955 a high school was established for grades nine through twelve.

The 1960s became a decade of change and turmoil. By 1959 the school had 139 students, but the school was beginning to change. The ethnic makeup of the area around the parish was becoming less Lithuanian and more Mexican, and Fr. Boreišis died. Some misunderstandings occurred between the parish council, the teachers, the parents, the principal, and the LB so that calls were made to change the place of the school. Also, another Saturday school began operating in 1962 under the leadership of the Knights of Lithuania with the support of the LB. They had 23 students to start off. The next year they were down to 17.[75]

A third Saturday school began in 1963 in Redford in the Arthur Vandenberg Public Elementary School. This school was run for four years by a parents' board in an apparent reaction to what was happening at St. Anthony's. It started with 43 students between kindergarten and seventh grades. This school was named after the great Lithuanian writer and patriot, Vincas Kudirka. One could consider this a split in the Detroit Lithuanian community. Apparently, the schools had a socioeconomic division and began to compete for students. Kudirka School was seen as "the doctors' school," while St. Anthony's was seen as the blue-collar school. Ironically, put together, the schools pulled in many more students than at any other time in the history of the Lithuanian community of Detroit. Between St. Anthony's Saturday school, now called Aušra ("Dawn" in English), and the Vincas Kudirka School, 210 students studied Lithuanian on Saturdays in the 1966–67 school year.[76] Including the Detroit schools, 3,199 Lithuanian-Americans attended forty-three Lithuanian primary Saturday schools across the United States in the 1966–67 school year, according to the LB.[77]

The combined eleventh and twelth grade classes of Lithuanian Saturday school in Southfield, Michigan in 1983–84.

Ultimately, because of finances, demographic changes, and the difficulty in obtaining educational sites (at one point Detroit Western High School was used), the schools chose to unite under one name, Lietuvių Bendruomenio Detroito Apylinkės Lituanistinės Mokykla (Lithuanian Community Detroit Area Lithuanian School). Yet, because the school was fourteen miles away in Redford, twenty-nine students returned to Aušra School. (Aušra folded in 1982.) This did not end the turmoil. Since most of the students attending the Redford school were not from Redford, the South Redford school board denied the use of the Vandenberg School. The Lithuanians in Redford created an organization, the Lithuanian Education Society of South Redford, of thirty-seven members in order to legally be allowed the use of the school.[78]

The school finally stabilized when the Lithuanian Cultural Center was built alongside the newly built Divine Providence Parish in Southfield in 1973. The school moved to the Cultural Center classrooms. The school had 118 students and added a logo and the name Žiburio ("Shining Light" in English).[79] The school remains at the Cultural Center to the present day. The student numbers are slowly diminishing, although new students have arrived from the fifth wave of immigration. The last time the high school reported graduates was in 1996, with two.[80] Teachers are also coming from fifth-wave ranks. Many of the teachers are graduates of the Lithuanian High School during the 1970s and 1980s.

For many students, after-school activities were conducted by the youth organizations: Ateitis or the Scouts. If a Lithuanian child of a third-wave immigrant grew up in Detroit, he or she was most likely in one of these two organizations. They were both major organizations in independent Lithuania and became the major youth organizations in Detroit. Very few joined both. By sixteen years of age, one had to commit to one organization or the other, but not both. Members from both organizations swore allegiance to God and country. Both had their official ideologies created in the 1930s by the Lithuanian philosopher Stasys Šalkauskis. From here, the focus was very different between the two and the history in independent Lithuania created a rift between the two.

The Ateitis organization was not supported by the government in Lithuania. In fact, to slow support, during high school it was illegal to join Ateitis. This was because many of the group's leaders became the leaders of the Christian Democratic Party, a rival to the authoritarian Nationalist regime of Antanas Smetona. President Smetona did allow the Scouts to remain as they were and in fact used them as a way to increase support for nationalism. Naturally, this political split repeated itself in third-wave immigrant life in Michigan. The Scouts created their regional groups, Baltija for the boys, and Gabija for the Girl Scouts. The Ateitis created their regional organization for the Detroit area.

A large difference between the two groups was religion. One main goal of the Ateitis organization was the fostering of Catholicism. One could not join this group if one were not Roman Catholic. Another main goal was intellectualism. When Ateitis groups met, they discussed religious and cultural issues. The Scouts worked on their program of badges. In the end, Ateitis has significantly declined in membership while the Scouts have maintained a status quo. It is interesting to note that the Scouts work toward creating an annual fair, Kazukio mugė, in March held at the Lithuanian Cultural Center gym, while the Ateitis groups have no such outreach activity. This dynamic may explain why some Lithuanian organizations wither and others maintain a degree of activity and membership.

Politics

The ultimate difference between the first two waves of Lithuanian immigration and the third wave was politics. As mentioned before, the more educated and politically aware third-wave immigrants worked relentlessly to use the political system to make American politicians understand the plight of Lithuania. This third wave was overwhelmingly Republican and for one simple fact: President Franklin Delano Roosevelt and his successor, President Truman, allowed the Soviet Union to incorporate Lithuania and the other Baltic countries. Lithuanians of the third wave lived in Germany, believing that independent countries before the war would remain independent after the war. This did not become reality and the third-wave immigrants blamed the Democratic presidents and their party for this failure.

Michigan, especially the Detroit area, became a major center of political activity among the national Lithuanian community. The organization with the largest impact on politics by Lithuanians in Michigan was the Jungtinis Amerikos Valstijos Lietuvių Bendruomenė (JAVLB), which translated means Lithuanian American Community. Lietuvos Bendruomenė created its first constitution at a gathering of Lithuanian displaced persons in Hanau, Germany, in March 1946. After some structural revision and definition, Lithuanians started organizing branches of the Lithuanian World Community, or Pasaulio Lietuvių Bendruomenė (PLB). The JAVLB branch was first organized in Chicago and New York in 1951, with the established arrival of the DP's. The indigent Lithuanian community looked upon this new organization as competition for long established organizations, societies, and clubs.[81] The Grand Rapids chapter was created in 1952 and the Detroit chapter in 1953. Lansing started a chapter, but there is no starting date given. The Detroit and Grand Rapids chapters of the LB (Lietuvių Bendruomenė or Lithuanian Community) are part of the Michigan Region of the JAVLB, which is a branch of the PLB.

The JAVLB established itself first as a cultural organization. The first governing board established a Cultural Fund, an Education Council, and a Cultural Information Bureau. The work in Lithuanian education by the LB in the United States and Michigan has already been documented with the establishment of Saturday schools in Grand Rapids and Detroit. The Education Council even today publishes textbooks and curricula, subsidizes schools, and organizes the Teachers' Week at Camp Dainava. The Cultural Fund supports Lithuanian language radio nationwide, including a program at Union Pier and one in Detroit. It also publishes books and periodicals, and organizes the Lithuanian Folk Dance Festival every four years, as well as a Lithuanian Song Festival.

These festivals play a vital part in keeping Lithuanian community life flourishing during the year. The organizational activity and the practices keep the Lithuanian culture alive in participants. Much like the sports festival, the dance festival allows Lithuanians of any descent, as well as spouses of non-descent, to participate in a cultural event that connects them with the larger world. Each Saturday school usually sends a group of schoolchildren to these festivals. The festivals publish a program book with a listing of members in each group with their picture. The last folk dance festival, the thirteenth, was held in Los Angeles, California, on July 3, 2008. The Sixth Folk Dance Festival in 1980 had the most participants, with 2,268 from all over the world. Detroit sent a primary school group, two high school groups, a university students' group, and a parents' group. Grand Rapids sent a group as well.

If two or more dance organizations exist within a city then competition puts pressure on each group to outperform the other. This is what happened with the high school groups in 1980. Galina Gobienė organized one of the groups, Šilainė, in 1949. The newer group, Audinys, led by Rusnė Kasputienė, was viewed as an upstart. Ultimately, Šilainė folded when Mrs. Gobienė retired. Sometime in the 1990s Mrs. Kasputis retired and Audinys folded as well. At the last folk festival only one high school group from Detroit, Šaltinis, led by Viktorija Viskantienė, participated. Detroit and Grand Rapids have always been apart of this LB-sponsored festival.

Politics became the unforeseen drive of the JAVLB. Through all these cultural events, the JAVLB had a way of keeping Lithuania in the minds of the American politicians. All these events drew local media. Naturally, politicians were invited and came in order to be seen with voters. For instance, Betty Ford attended the fifth Lithuanian Folk Dance Festival, held in Chicago in 1976. Next to her was the governor of Illinois, Dan Walker. The program director for the festival was Mrs. Guobienė. The 1980 dance festival had Mayor Jayne Byrne and Congressman Edward Derwinski in attendance. President Reagan and House Speaker Tip O'Neill both sent letters to the festival that were published in the festival's program guidebook.[82]

Note how Republican and Democrat politicians alike tried to win the Lithuanian vote. The JAVLB had found a way to get support from both parties at the national level for the simple reason that Lithuania's cause is a foreign diplomacy issue, an issue held within executive power. Therefore the JAVLB had to find ways to get access to the executive branch without showing the Republican character of the third wave.

As a solution to this problem, the JAVLB help set up a Baltic Caucus within the U.S. House of Representatives and the U.S. Senate. This caucus was created in 1997 and is chaired by Republican Representative John Shimkus from Illinois and Democratic Representative Dennis Kucinich from Ohio. Twelve of the sixteen Michigan Representatives have joined the Baltic Caucus, four Democrats and eight Republicans. Democratic Senator Richard Durbin from Illinois and Republican Senator Gordon Smith from Oregon co-chair the Senate Baltic Caucus. Democratic Senator Debbie Stabenow from Michigan has also joined this caucus. The Baltic Caucus makes decisions on how American policy can best help the Lithuanian, Latvian, and Estonian causes. Each chapter within the JAVLB, with regional help, works to persuade their state representatives to join the Baltic Caucus. Michigan Lithuanians and the other Balts of Michigan have done well, as a majority of the state's federal legislative branch have chosen to join the Baltic Caucus. especially as compared to states like Illinois, which has only five of its twenty House delegates on the Baltic Caucus.

The political work does not end with the Baltic Caucus. The Detroit District of the JAVLB has been able to consistently bring in American and Lithuanian politicians to meetings sponsored by the Detroit LB. American politicians who have attended programs at the Lithuanian Cultural Center connected to Divine Providence Parish include U.S. Senators Donald Riegle Jr., Robert Griffin, and Spencer Abraham and U.S. Representatives Dick Chrysler, Joe Knollenberg, and William Broomfield. Michigan Governors Blanchard and Engler have attended activities there as well. Lithuanian politicians who have attended these activities include "Sąjudis" leader and later president of Lithuania, Vytautas Landsbergis; Lithuania's ambassador to the United States, Stasys Lozoraitis; and presidents of the PLB like Vytautas Kamantas, Dr. Vytautas Bieliauskas, Bronius Nainys; and Presidents of the JAVLB, including Dr. Antanas Razma, Vytautas Kutkus, Algimantas Gečys, and Vytautas Volertas. By politicizing many of the cultural events organized by the Detroit LB, American politicians and the Lithuanian émigré community in the greater Detroit area keep Lithuania's political environment in the public eye.

Beyond organizational politics, many individuals who grew up in Detroit have become powerful people in politics. Jonas Urbonas has been a tireless organizer of Lithuanian Republicans in the Detroit area. His influence has been felt on the younger generation, who have campaigned for the Republican Party in the Detroit suburbs. The most notable of these politicians is Saulius Anužis. He has worked in Lansing at the state level for over two decades. He managed State Senator Posthumus's campaign. Mr. Anužis has worked his way up the Michigan Republican Party chain to become its party chairman in February 2005. He also serves as honorary consul to Michigan for the Republic of Lithuania as well as the Lansing LB chapter president.[83]

Gintė Damušytė, daughter of Adolfas and Jadvyga Damušiene, worked her way through foreign politics to become Lithuania's ambassador to Austria, moving to ambassador to NATO, and today she is ambassador to Canada. She became politically active as a teen and worked in the Lithuanian Information Center in Brooklyn, New York. She held that post for many years and when Lithuania became independent, her political experience in the international arena allowed her these opportunities. She has lived the third-wave immigrant's dream of returning to Lithuania. Her parents also moved to Lithuania.

The fact that U.S. Senator Donald Riegle Jr. visited the Lithuanian Cultural Center should not be surprising, since Violeta Abarius worked for him as a case worker. She went along with Ginté Damušyté and two other Michigan Lithuanian natives, Viktoras Nakas and Asta Banionyté, to Washington, D.C. There this group of immigrants' children carried on the work of their parents by saving the Lithuanian embassy to the United States. The embassy was to be closed due to the United States' regulations for embassies. Violeta Abarius edited a newsletter and the group persuaded five thousand people to show up for a demonstration. The embassy was saved. She returned to Michigan to graduate from the University of Michigan. She helped organize a demonstration of Lithuanians at Kennedy Square, Detroit, in 1977. She then became president of the World Lithuanian Youth Congress in 1979. She helped organize thousands of delegates who traveled across the Midwest holding meetings for a few days at a time in each place, starting at Oberlin College and ending in Montreal. When this was completed, she began work for Senator Riegle, retiring from politics in the mid-1980s.[84]

In the end, third-wave Lithuanian immigrants were more politically aware than their first- and second-wave colleagues. The political awareness was born out of necessity to keep the hope alive that Lithuania would be independent some day. The political nature of that goal meant that Lithuanians in Michigan had to be outward looking. They could not afford to get caught in partisan politics, for fear of losing executive support. The third-wave Lithuanian immigrants did an excellent job of creating a system that connected Lithuanian colonies through cultural festivals and kept the political situation in the minds of the Lithuanian community and the American politicians. The Lithuanian Community was not solely responsible for this, but was instrumental. Lithuanian-born immigrants set up a system that got their children involved in Lithuanian diplomacy as well. Since the goal of Lithuanian independence has been achieved, the organizational complex set up by third-wave immigrants has continued the work of keeping Lithuanian culture alive by extending its goals to help Lithuania in many ways as well as continuing its work here in the United States and Michigan.

The differences between the first- and second-wave immigrants and those of the third wave are vast. Although they all came from the same country, their sociological differences and their reasons for coming to the United States were different. First- and second-wave immigrants never intended to return to Lithuania. Although they created schools and organizations to keep their Lithuanian heritage alive, the reality for them was gradual assimilation. Some fought it, but not with the same intensity and focus seen in the third-wave immigrants. The ultimate goal for the third-wave immigrant was return to an independent Lithuania. This goal preordained the tone of their immigration. They fought assimilation as much as possible. This difference created a dissonance between the first- and second-wave immigrants and the third-wave immigrants. Third-wave immigrants tried to take over the organizations set up by first- and second-wave Lithuanians. When this could not be done, third-wave immigrants created their own organizations built on their experiences in Lithuania and the DP camps. The third-wave organizations were more centralized and focused, while first- and second-wave organizations were divergent and scattered, with many overlapping goals and services. Maybe the large numbers of first- and second-wave immigrants precluded any kind of centralization. In the end, first- and second-wave organizations have been receding in membership and power, while third-wave organizations have flourished, though some receded in some respects when the goal of Lithuanian independence was attained. Yet these organizations have so far been able to recruit younger Lithuanians to take over leadership roles and assimilate the new wave of immigrants.

The Fourth Wave

T he fourth wave of immigration to Michigan concerns those Lithuanians who left Soviet controlled Lithuania between the end of the displaced persons immigration in 1953 and the renewal of independence in 1991. No statistics could be found showing the number of Lithuanians who moved to Michigan during this time. The author remembers a couple of people who did make the sacrifice to move to the West and live in the Detroit area. Leaving the Soviet Union to live abroad was a difficult task, filled with political pitfalls. Very few visas for visiting purposes were granted and fewer still for emigration purposes.

In general, fourth-wave immigrants were viewed with some suspicion. Rumors among third-wave immigrants were based on the perception that nobody got out of the USSR without having "political connections," meaning "ties to the Soviet secret police, the KGB." Obviously, their small numbers meant they made little impact on the life of Lithuanians in Michigan. The attitude of third-wave immigrants toward the fourth-wave immigrants became a portent of the relationship to come between third-wave immigrants and those of the larger fifth wave.

The Fifth Wave of Immigration and Today

On March 11, 1990, the Lithuanian Soviet Socialist Republic declared its independence from the Union of Soviet Socialist Republics. Recognition was not forthcoming from the USSR or the rest of the world. The failed Soviet coup in August 1991 led to Western recognition and finally a Soviet ratification of independence in September 1991. Lithuania S.S.R. was now the Republic of Lithuania. This event was earth shaking to the Lithuanian émigrés abroad, including those in Michigan. For Lithuanians of the third wave, recognition of Lithuanian independence by the United States had a "Where were you when Lithuania got its independence?" affect.[85] By the end of the year a realization struck every third-wave immigrant who had struggled for Lithuania's cause: the goal was achieved and the work was done. Now what? People did not know what to do. Nobody foresaw that the goal of independence would be achieved in such a quick and peaceful manner. Therefore, a post-independence blueprint for the Lithuanian immigrant community had not been designed. The émigré community was left searching for some useful goal.

At the very least, active Lithuanian Michiganders had to see for themselves the free and democratic Lithuania. Then, presumably, the next step would be more apparent. Many third-wave immigrants, now retired, went back to Lithuania and lived there. The young at least visited and some

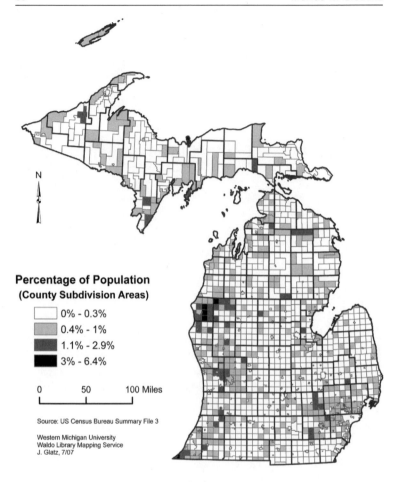

Percentage of Population
(County Subdivision Areas)

- ☐ 0% - 0.3%
- ▨ 0.4% - 1%
- ▩ 1.1% - 2.9%
- ■ 3% - 6.4%

0   50   100 Miles

Source: US Census Bureau Summary File 3

Western Michigan University
Waldo Library Mapping Service
J. Glatz, 7/07

stayed, usually for philanthropic reasons or to further their education. Some tried to spread capitalism by trying to open a business. Others in the United States shortsightedly believed that the émigré community would wither into nothing as the mission of freedom, around which most of the Lithuanian-American organizational complex had been built, was accomplished. After many had visited Lithuania, what became apparent to Lithuanians in Michigan was that the second generation of third-wave immigrants was facing an identity crisis.

This identity crisis had its origin in the reasons for their parents leaving Lithuania in the first place. All through their education as Lithuanians, the children of the third-wave immigrants were taught that they were 100 percent Lithuanian. The implicit message was that they would return to Lithuania to carry on the torch of Lithuanianism, as if the Lithuanians in Lithuania were not Lithuanian enough. Many second-generation third-wave Lithuanians were confused by the reception they received when visiting their homeland. Lithuanians were the real Lithuanians and the third-wavers and their children were not. Third-wavers had become Americans. Young Lithuanian-Americans were in a limbo, while their parents focused on regaining their political rights in Lithuania.

The third-wave Lithuanian immigrants who had arrived in America in the late 1940s and early 1950s now lobbied for past political rights to be recognized in the newly independent Lithuania. These Lithuanian-Americans wanted to be able to reclaim their land in Lithuania. Many of them had kept their deeds since the 1930s. They lobbied for a return of citizenship, since many had kept their passports since the debacle in 1939. Some wanted to run for office. In the end, the government in Lithuania capitulated on almost all accounts (though deeds were not fully recognized as proving ownership).

The biggest connection to Michigan in all this political activity was Valdas Adamkus. Valdas Adamkus was born in Lithuania. He left Lithuania and came to the United States as a DP. He became college educated, worked to become the head of the Great Lakes Region for the U.S. Environmental Protection Agency by the 1990s, and lived in Chicago. While in the United States, he invested his organizational skills in the Lithuanian émigré community. He was key to keeping the Lithuanian athletic movement in North America vibrant, and organized the first World Lithuanian Games, played in Toronto in 1978. Valdas Adamkus was also the owner of Tabor Farms in Sodus, Michigan. (Some Lithuanians believe "Sodus" to be a Lithuanian-named village because "sodas" means "orchard" in Lithuanian. This is not the case.) A Lithuanian named Juozas Bachunas originally owned Tabor Farms. Tabor Farms was a resort for Lithuanians, usually of the Nationalist/Sandara Organization. The exiled president of Lithuania, Antanas Smetona, himself a *tautininkas* (Nationalist Party member), stayed at Tabor Farms in 1941 for five months. Valdas Adamkus was a member of this organization. When Mr. Bachunas died in 1967, he left Tabor Farms to Valdas Adamkus.

Later Adamkus sold the resort, making millions of dollars. The profit was part of what allowed Mr. Adamkus to return to Lithuania and make a successful bid for the presidency in 1998. In a sense, a piece of Michigan real estate enabled a third-wave Lithuanian immigrant to move to Lithuania, run a nationwide campaign, and become its president. The "American Dream" had its impact on Lithuania.

The children of third-wave immigrants felt more ambiguous in their position as Lithuanians than did their parents by the time the fifth wave of Lithuanians entered the United States. Soon after their arrival, the fifth-wavers started to join in existing Lithuanian cultural groups or start their own organizations. Young third-wavers saw this as a threat. The more Lithuanians immigrated to the United States, the less power third-wavers seemed to have in the organizations built by their parents and grandparents. In response, young third-wavers began to use a semi-derogatory term, "waynians," as in "Lithu-waynians," to denote fifth-wave immigrants.

One contributor to the generational differences between the third- and fifth-wave immigrants is the differences between the Soviet Lithuanian culture and the American Lithuanian culture. Cultures never stay the same, no matter how much work is put into conserving them. Culture is always moving and changing. The result can be illustrated in a number of ways. First, the third-wave immigrants built and insulated many of their organizations against the natural cultural change. The Lithuanian culture they tried to conserve was that of the 1930s. Books published in the United States about Lithuania and used in Lithuanian Saturday schools had pictures from Lithuania during the preceding period of independence. The songs taught were composed in that time period or before. If new songs were composed, they were about the romantic longing for the old Lithuania. Every child could recite or sing the Lithuanian Anthem from the independent years. The famous people looked up to and written about were from that time period or before. Lithuanian religious holidays were important to observe. Lithuanian Christmas ornaments made of straw (drinking straws were used instead of the field hay they used in the Old Country) were hung and eggs were painted with old pagan symbols using candle wax for Easter. To third-wave immigrants and their children, Lithuanian history and culture stopped in 1939, when Lithuania was finally occupied by the Soviets. Sure, Lithuanians in the United States started to eat hamburgers and fries, listen to rock and roll, and use Lithuanianized English, but even with these encroachments of American culture, the Lithuanian culture taught and learned was essentially that of the 1930s.

While Lithuanian Michiganders were engrained with 1930s Lithuanian culture, the culture in Lithuania remained more open and free to the environment around them. Lithuanians in the Soviet Union dropped certain aspects of Lithuanian culture that seemed outdated and useless. They did not have Lithuanian folk dancing as a class from kindergarten to twelfth grade, as Lithuanian-Americans did. That kind of "stuff" was for cultural historians. They sang new communist songs. They didn't learn the old Lithuanian Anthem. Christmas and Easter were barely a thought to the new atheist environment. As Russians moved into Lithuania and Lithuanians moved to other parts of the Soviet Union and returned, Lithuanians adopted different words and spellings. They even used Lithuanianized English on public signs (perhaps as a form of dissent), while this same type of language was looked down upon by third-wave immigrants in the United States.[86] When young Lithuanian-Americans tried to communicate with the new Lithuanian immigrants, they did not connect culturally. They were literally from two different eras.

Besides the cultural differences between the immigrants, the question of illegal immigration follows the fifth wave. When a fifth-wave Lithuanian arrives to a community in Michigan, the question of illegal immigration arises within the third-wave immigrant's mind. During sports events, where all Lithuanians are invited to participate, some third-wavers have questioned the legitimacy of fifth-wavers' participation because of immigration status. A young anonymous Lithuanian wrote a short essay to the Lithuanian magazine, *Ateitis* (The Future), describing her harrowing experience when immigrating to the Detroit area. She had to endure all the problems of illegal entrance into the United States by going to Mexico and then crossing the Mexican-U.S. border. Ultimately she ended up in Michigan, living a successful life, but her story is all-too-familiar to fifth-wave immigrants, and this creates suspicion among the older immigrants.[87]

The Union Pier Experience

The cultural dissonance between the third and fifth immigrant waves has resulted in a cooperative development in one Michigan community. Union Pier, on the far southern end of Lake Michigan, has been home to a small Lithuanian community since the late 1950s that has gone through patterns of growth and decline. Today the Union Pier Lithuanian community is in a period of growth, with both third-wavers and fifth-wave immigrants moving in.

Before Union Pier became a Lithuanian community, it was a Jewish summer community. Jews had owned many of the homes since the 1920s. In the late 1950s they started to move on and sold their cottages to Lithuanians from Chicago. Union Pier became the new summer resort area for Lithuanians who did not have a chance to buy the cottages at Beverly Shores, Indiana. Enough Lithuanians bought homes at Union Pier to start a Lithuanian homeowners association to protect their interests. Coming primarily from Chicago, the Lithuanian population would swell in the summers with third-wave immigrants. Resort Gintaras (Lithuanian for "amber") was opened in Union Pier in 1960 by the parents of the current owner, Gintaras Karaitis. At that time, the resort allowed only Lithuanian clientele. Lithuanian clubs from Chicago would sponsor dances at Resort Gintaras throughout the summer. The popularity of this resort allowed for Lithuanian Catholic Masses to be held during the summer and for donations to be raised for Lithuanian social organizations.

Invariably, the Lithuanian community at Union Pier dealt with the same stagnation faced by other Lithuanian communities in Michigan. The decrease in activity began in the 1970s. As the economy soured, the Lithuanian population became older, and the younger generation had different interests, Union Pier became less popular. Fewer people came to the dances, and as a result, fewer dances were sponsored. Lithuanians died away or sold their cottages and homes. Resort Gintaras survived, but began to take in non-Lithuanian guests. By the 1980s, only one Lithuanian picnic was held each year and Masses were no longer offered on weekends. The Lithuanian youth of the Midwest were interested in Union Pier only two times a year: Memorial Day and Labor Day weekends. On these weekends the youth would make a pilgrimage to the shores of Lake Michigan for a seventy-two-hour party. The parties were open, so the organizational/ideological delineations that held sway during the rest of the year were forgotten for the holiday weekend. Other than these two weekends, however, Union Pier appeared to have become somewhat of a Lithuanian ghost colony.[88]

Today, the Lithuanian community at Union Pier has been revitalized. Young third-wave Chicago-area Lithuanian-American families with children are moving to Union Pier to stay all year round. About forty fifth-wave Lithuanian immigrants have moved to Union Pier. A Lithuanian Sea Scouts troop was established in the fall of 2002. The community has organized a movement to create a Lithuanian Saturday school, so that the families will no longer have to carpool the hour and a half to Chicago or Lemont, Illinois. A three-day Heritage Camp has been created for area youth that is so successful that youngsters have been turned away.[89] The most promising developments have been the opening of two stores for year-round service and the addition of a Lithuanian realtor, who decorates her advertising in the colors of the Lithuanian flag: yellow, green, and red.

Union Pier is successfully creating an atmosphere of cooperation between the third-wave immigrant children and the fifth-wave immigrants. The cooperation lies in cultural events. The fifth-wave immigrants understand that they are lacking in the "lost" traditions of the handmade arts of Lithuania. The heritage camp and community meetings during Thanksgiving, Christmas, and Easter allow the third-wave immigrants to teach the fifth-wave

Milda's Corner Store

Milda Rudaitis is a member of the new wave of Lithuanians coming to Michigan via Chicago. Although Milda grew up in the center of Lithuanian activity in Marquette Park, Chicago, she has become successful in Michigan by using her ethnographic expertise at her store, Milda's Corner Store in Union Pier. She was born in Chicago to a second-wave Lithuanian mother and a third-wave Lithuanian father. She graduated from Morton West High School in Berwyn, Illinois, but she also spent a year attending the only full-time Lithuanian high school outside of Lithuania, based in Germany, the V16 or *Vasario 16ta* (February Sixteenth, named for Lithuania's independence day). She joined Lithuanian youth groups in Chicago. She also attended and graduated from the Lithuanian Saturday school in Marquette Park, as well as the Lithuanian Pedagogical Institute. She finished her education with a degree in culinary arts from Kendall College in Evanston, Illinois. Her store is successful because her Lithuanian cultural heritage connects to the Lithuanians of the first through the fifth waves in the area but also to the other cultures that have established themselves in the Union Pier area, like Jews, Latvians, and Slovaks. Her delicatessen features foods these ethnic people relate to, like kugelis, koldūnai (progies in Polish), and beet soup. She also sells products from Lithuania, such as canned mushrooms. At her store she teaches ethnographic arts, like Easter egg design.

immigrants the conserved 1930s Lithuanian culture. They have classes in making straw Christmas ornaments and Lithuanian decorated Easter eggs. The community is bringing more fifth-wave immigrants into the third-wave community.[90]

Union Pier is also finding success in the Lithuanian acculturation of the Union Pier American community. One of area the businesses is a Lithuanian deli owned by a third-wave immigrant child, Milda Rudaitis. She bakes and sells Lithuanian food like kugelis (see recipe), koldūnai (progies, in Polish), and šaltibarščiai (cold beet soup). She also makes traditional Christmas meals in December and sells products from Lithuania. Surprisingly, Americans buy the products. The Jewish community especially likes the food.[91] This is not surprising, since one of the ethnic groups that emigrated with Lithuanians from Russia were the Jews. The Lithuanian community at Union Pier seems to have found a way to work with the new immigrants and renew itself without a Lithuanian parish center nearby.

Outside of Union Pier, the energy within the old Lithuanian communities of Saginaw, Albion, Jackson, Painesdale, and Lake and Mason counties has dissipated. The standard difficulties stand behind this phenomenon. Suburbanization makes meeting with the community inconvenient. Marriage into American families creates feelings of betrayal for hard-core Lithuanian immigrants. Immigrant children feel forced to leave the native Lithuanian community for better and more opportunities elsewhere. Assimilation has made casualties of the Michigan Lithuanian colonies.

The proof of these causes can be found in any phonebook from these areas. There are a handful of Lithuanian names in the Houghton phonebook of 2001, where a mining community of about sixty lived. The 1999 Manistee area phonebook, used for Mason and Lake counties, shows only twenty-nine Lithuanian names that also show up on the cemetery records from those counties. The lists of six cemeteries from the Manistee area show 105 different Lithuanian names.[92] This means that almost three-quarters of all Lithuanian names from the Mason County area have disappeared. One must also look at the number of entries per name in the phonebook. Only five of the twenty-nine names have more than one or two entries. A handful of Lithuanian names are found in the phonebook that are not in the cemetery records, but not enough to make up for the decimated ranks previously described. These are just two examples, proving the dissipation of two communities. The casualty rate in the other communities is probably not much better, even if cities like Detroit and Grand Rapids have larger Lithuanian populations.

Parish closings and the difficulty of finding Lithuanian parish priests also provide evidence of the communities' decline. The mass closing of Catholic parishes in the Detroit Archdiocese in 1989 did not leave Lithuanians unaffected. Plans to close Lithuanian parishes were made. St. Peter's Lithuanian Parish was closed in 1995 because of declining numbers and the lack of a Lithuanian priest. St. Anthony's Lithuanian Parish will be closed as soon as the current priest passes away or retires. These closings will leave the Detroit area with only one Lithuanian parish, Divine Providence (in Southfield).

While the Lithuanian parishes in Detroit were being closed, Divine Providence Parish was dealing with its own problems. Fr. Kriščiunevičius retired in 1995, leaving no Lithuanian replacement. Without the knowledge of parishioners, the archdiocese advertised an opening for the church without requiring the priest to speak Lithuanian. The position was filled by a non-Lithuanian priest. The parishioners had to scramble to find a Lithuanian-speaking priest. They found a Soviet-era Lithuanian born and ordained priest named Fr. Valdas Valdemaras.

In less than a year, Fr. Valdas's pastorship became rocked by financial controversy. Fr. Valdemaras was spending large amounts of money without authorization from the Parish Council. After complaints from the council, Fr. Valdemaras dissolved the council. At least three different sets of parish leaders tried to get a working relationship going. All attempts failed. Fr. Valdas would not budge. The council, despite being officially dissolved, kept working and communicating with the parishioners. In the end, Fr. Valdemaras was relieved of his duties, but only after a concerted lobbying effort by parishioners to the local bishops and the archbishop. The parish was once again scrambling to find a Lithuanian priest, except now the archbishop had even more reason to get the ethnic stipulation changed to geographic![93]

In the end, Divine Providence found a trustworthy and capable pastor in another Soviet-era Lithuanian born and ordained priest, Fr. Aloyzas Volskis. His leadership has steadied the community. Yet, the controversy had a social cost. The parish became divided between those supporting Fr. Valdas, those trying to find a working relationship with him, and those who wanted him out. At the very least these hard feelings between parishioners will make cooperation a little more difficult now that the controversy has subsided.

Today Divine Providence is at least slowing the hemorrhaging of members. Fifth- wave immigrants are taking the place of deceased or assimilated members. Cultural organizations are staying active. After the Sunday morning Lithuanian Mass, new immigrants sell Lithuanian food for a reasonable price in the parish hall. The post-Mass socializing allows suburbanized Lithuanian immigrants of all waves to spend some informal time together, outside of the politically charged organizations previously mentioned. The small successes at Union Pier and Detroit with fifth-wave immigrants brings up the question, "Can Lithuanian colonies sustain, or even improve their vitality?"

The most telling answer to this question is the religious health of the Lithuanian communities in Michigan. Since the beginning of Lithuanian communities in Michigan, priests have been the human focus of Lithuanian activity. Priests were the impetus for the start of Lithuanian parishes and later Lithuanian schools and cultural centers. Priests are expected to attend Lithuanian activities. Having a Lithuanian priest at family gatherings or social activities is an honor. Every organization had a position named the spiritual leader (*dvasinis vadas*) and filled by the priest. If Lithuanian priests are seen less and less, then the health of the Lithuanian community is in question.

Camp Dainava is a prime example of this reality. Priests helped found the camp. No camping group had problems finding a Lithuanian priest to spend his vacation with the groups so that daily masses could be celebrated. For many years, Fr. Viktoras Dabušis was the camp administrator and lived on the campgrounds during the summers. Detroiters coming to visit the camp for the day could count on at least one Sunday mass in the morning, another in the evening for the incoming campers, and sometimes even a third mass, if mass at Pilėnai was offered. By the early 1990s this had all changed. Groups struggled to find priests to join in the camps. Priests rarely stayed during their vacations. Detroit priests no longer came to offer mass, unless for the annual picnic. By the summer of 2003, the Heritage Camp could not find a Lithuanian priest who would come for the two Sundays. The camp coordinator had to call local parishes to find an available priest. A parish from Ann Arbor allowed their visiting Nigerian priest to celebrate mass. This was certainly a first in Camp Dainava history!

The statistics show the stress on the Lithuanian religious community. The Lithuanian communities in Michigan had forty-one Lithuanian priests in 1953. Many of these priests were sons of immigrants or newly immigrated DP's. Many of these worked in geographic parishes, not just Lithuanian parishes. By 1979, the number of Lithuanian priests had dropped to twenty-six. That's a 37 percent drop in twenty-six years. As far as is known, no new priests from Lithuanian communities have been ordained since then. As with Divine Providence, retirements, as well as parish closings and deaths, have dropped the numbers even further. If Lithuanian culture in Michigan is to survive, parishes need to increase religious vocations. Priests need to be actively fostered and supported from within the Lithuanian community itself. The Lithuanian priesthood in Michigan has declined as has the priesthood across Michigan, but with the added dynamics of assimilation in the immigrant community, the religious health, and therefore the cultural health of the Lithuanian community has been weakened severely in recent years.

The Future of Lithuanians in Michigan

The Lithuanian community in Michigan will survive in Detroit for some time to come, as long as economic opportunity and Lithuanian priests exist. Some older Lithuanian immigrants have their doubts, however. One older immigrant believes that Lithuanians in Detroit will not last much longer than 2015. This person's prophecy is based on the prediction that the Lithuanian parishes will lose membership, lose their Lithuanian priest, and close. Another immigrant predicts that within twenty years the church will become geographic and fall under total local episcopal control and this will be the end of the Lithuanian influence on the community. This has happened to other Lithuanian communities in Michigan. Assimilation is too doggedly persistent a force to be staved off into the future.

The process of assimilation is unrelenting. The immigrant generation can survive with its linguistic, religious, and social base intact. However as the second generation moves into the dominant culture and attends school, the process of assimilation sets in. This is especially true for a small group like the Lithuanians. New friends are made and marriage outside the ethnic community makes serious inroads.

At the very least, in order to survive, a Lithuanian community in Michigan must have some challenge larger than itself to keep the collective focus. That focus cannot be to keep itself Lithuanian. Lithuanianism has to be used to achieve a greater good, rather than to keep itself alive. With this in mind, Kovas would be one of the last organizations to survive. The athletic club always will have an annual goal of competing with other clubs from other Lithuanian colonies. Furthermore, the medical goal of helping children in Lithuania through the American-Lithuanian Disability and Rehabilitation Exchange Program or the political goal of getting Lithuania permanent NATO status would be goals worthy to sustain the Lithuanian community. A lot more goals in this vein need to be organized to inspire a continuation of Lithuanianism.

For these larger goals to be organized and achieved, a regular, central meeting place must be physically available. The Lithuanian parish has always been *the* integral part of the Lithuanian immigrant landscape in providing a familiar gathering space (along with its religious function). The survival of the Lithuanian parish is equal to the survival of the Lithuanian community and culture. As the Lithuanian parish goes, so does the Lithuanian culture. The proof can be seen in the Lithuanian communities outside of Detroit and Grand Rapids, such as those in Saginaw and Custer (New Lithuania). Saginaw and Custer used to have parishes, but no longer do, and the Lithuanian culture in these areas is practically extinct.

As seen with the past waves of Lithuanian immigration, usually an influx of large numbers of Lithuanians helps to reinvigorate the life of the Lithuanian community. New immigrants come with ties to the old country that can be positively exploited to keep Lithuanianism alive in the colony and improve lives in Lithuania. The Detroit colony has this potential today. The older colonies in out-state Michigan do not look healthy, save for Union Pier. They have separated themselves from some greater goal, especially since Lithuania became independent of the Soviet Union in 1991, and new immigrants from Lithuania have not arrived in sufficient numbers to make a difference. They are being assimilated into the American cultural landscape one person at a time.

Conclusion

ithuanians have been a part of the Michigan historical landscape since they first arrived in the 1870s. They may have been few in number compared to other ethnic groups, but Lithuanians survived in Michigan and made an impact in all areas of the state. Lithuanians logged, mined, farmed, and built furniture and cars. They built Lithuanian neighborhoods and parishes and the support groups that go with them. Lithuanians in Michigan today are working in new industries such as tourism and medicine. They created recreational camps to get the Lithuanians of the Midwest region to meet during summers and holidays in order to discuss issues of importance to all Lithuanians, not just those in Michigan. As long as new Lithuanian immigrants arrive in Michigan to replenish the assimilated or deceased and make a positive impact, especially in the religious sphere, then the Lithuanian community will survive in Michigan.

Appendix 1

Lithuanian Recipes

Kugelis (Potato Cake)

4 lbs. finely grated potatoes
1 medium onion, finely chopped
2 eggs slightly beaten
½ lb. bacon chopped and browned
¼ c. farina or Cream of Wheat
½ c. flour
¼ lb. of butter
1 small can of evaporated milk
½ tsp. of salt
1 or 2 tablets of ground Vitamin C to keep grated potatoes white
(*optional*)

Mix all the ingredients together until they are spread equally throughout, and pour into a two-inch deep 14" × 10" pan.

Heat, uncovered, in a 400° Fahrenheit oven for one hour. Reduce heat to 350° for a second hour. Kugelis is done when the cook can stick a toothpick into the center of the cake and pull it out without any batter sticking to it. Also, the sides should be a deep brown and starting to pull away from the pan near the top.

This recipe serves 6 to 8 people. Cut in squares and eat with sour cream on top. Also, one may top with sautéed bacon, mushrooms, or onions.

This is my Grandmother Stasė Tumosa's recipe.

Kisielius (Christmas Cranberry Pudding)

½ gallon of cranberry juice

½ gallon of water (reserve 1 cup)

½ c. sugar

1 cinnamon stick

¼ box of potato starch (corn starch may be used as a substitute)

Mix everything together except for the starch and the reserved water, and bring to a boil.

Dilute the starch in the reserved (cold) water in a three- or four-cup measuring cup.

Slowly add the starch mixture to the boiled mixture and mix in completely, until the pudding is pudding thick (or to cook's preference).

Cool at room temperature until the cook can pour the pudding into a glass serving bowl.

Chill in the refrigerator. Decorate with dried fruits.

Add more dried fruits or *parpeliukai/šližikai* when eating.

This is my Grandmother Stasė Tumosa's recipe.

Lithuanian Organizations

- **ALRKF Camp Dainava**, 15100 West Austin Road, Manchester, MI 48158. A small library is found on the second floor meeting room in the Dr. Adolfas Damušis Dormitory.

- **Balzekas Museum of Lithuanian Culture**, 6500 South Pulaski Road, Chicago, IL 60629. For a registration fee, a person may research topics in their substantial library.

- **Divine Providence Roman Catholic Church (Lithuanian)**, Nine Mile Road, Southfield, MI 48033. The Lithuanian Cultural Center is connected to the church. The Lithuanian Saturday school, bookstore (books sold after Lithuanian Mass on Sundays), meeting hall, stage, and gym are part of this cultural center.

- **Immigration History Research Center**, 826 Berry Street, Minneapolis, MN 55114. Located at the University of Minnesota, this is a valuable library and archival resource on eastern and southern Europeans, including Lithuanians. In addition to serials and newspapers, the center has a large holding of books and monographs on the immigrant community, along with archival resources and manuscripts.

- **Lithuanian American Cultural Archives**, Thurber Road, Putnam, CT 06260. Run by the Lithuanian Marian Fathers, this organization has an extensive collection of early materials on the immigrant community, especially on Lithuanians in the Northeast and Middle Atlantic states.

■ **Lithuanian Museum**, 5620 South Claremont Avenue, Chicago, IL 60636. Founded to promote and further an understanding of the Lithuanian American immigrant experience, the museum sponsors both permanent and traveling exhibits and also houses a library. The Lithuanian Museum is affiliated with the World Lithuanian Archives, a major repository of materials by and about the Lithuanian American community, gathered by the Lithuanian Jesuit Fathers Provincial House in Chicago.

Notes

1. In 1905, the Polish writer Henryk Sienkiewicz won the Nobel Prize for Literature, partly for his historical fiction about the Battle of Tannenburg titled *The Teutonic Knights* (first printed in 1900). In this epic he depicted the Lithuanians as very uncivilized.

2. Alfonsas Eidintas, *Lithuanian Emigration to the United States: 1868–1950*, trans. Thomas A. Michalski (Vilnius, Lithuania: Mokslo ir enciklopedijų leidybos institutas, 2003), 52–53. See also David Fainhauz, *Lithuanians in the USA: Aspects of Ethnic Identity*, trans. Algirdas Dumcius (Chicago: Library Press, 1991), 14.

3. Edward V. Gillis, *Growing Up in Old Lithuanian Town* (Grand Rapids, Mich.: Grand Rapids Historical Commission, 2001), 3.

4. Balys Raugas, ed. *JAV LB Trys Dešimtmečiai* (Jungtinių Amerikos Valstybių Lietuvių Bendruomenės Krašto Valdyba, 1982), 92.

5. Gillis, *Growing Up in Old Lithuanian Town*, 3.

6. Vl. Pauža, "Detroitas," *Lietuvių Enciklopedija*, vol. 4, ed. Vaclovas Biržiška (South Boston, Mass.: Lietuvių enciklopedijos leidykla, 1954), 474. See also Anicetas Simutis, ed., *Pasaulio Lietuvių Žinynas* [Lithuanian World Directory]. (New York: Lithuanian Chamber of Commerce, 1958), 304.

7. Eidintas, *Lithuanian Emigration to the United States*, 60–61.

8. Ibid., 150–51.

9. Ibid., 24.

10. Victor Greene, *For God and Country: The Rise of Polish and Lithuanian Ethnic Consciousness in America, 1860–1910*, (Madison, Wisc.: State Historical Society of Wisconsin, 1975), 37–38.

11. Fainhauz, *Lithuanians in the USA*, 19.

12. Pauža, "Detroitas," 474.

13. Simutis, *Pasaulio Lietuvių Žinynas*, 144.

14. "Selected Population Data for Detroit and Michigan," in *Telling Detroit's Story* (Detroit: Detroit 300, 2001), 191.

15. Gillis, *Growing Up in Old Lithuanian Town*, 32–33.

16. Peter Gavrilovich and Bill McGraw, eds., *The Detroit Almanac: 300 Years of Life in the Motor City* (Detroit: Detroit Free Press, 2001), 166.

17. Willis F. Dunbar and George S. May, *Michigan: A History of the Wolverine State*, 3rd ed. (Grand Rapids, Mich.: Eerdmans, 1995), 361.

18. Eidintas, *Lithuanian Emigration to the United States*, 25.

19. In 1998–99, a group of Lithuanian-Americans created a set of websites documenting Lithuanian cemeteries in Michigan and Lithuanians in Michigan from the 1920 U.S. Census. This website must be used cautiously. The incomplete transcription of the 1920 Census lists 2,493 Lithuanians, of the 5,556 shown to be living in Michigan in the Census. All of the major colonies are reported in order of size: Detroit; Grand Rapids; Mason, Lake, and Oceana Counties; Saginaw; Hamtramck; Houghton County; and Jackson. Thirty-six other locations throughout the state are given as places of residence, including nine of the fifteen counties in the Upper Peninsula. It also documents the jobs these people held, whether they were married, and the size of their family. "1920 Michigan Census," Lithuanian Global Genealogical Society website: www.angelfire.com/mi/lithgen/1920.html (accessed August 13, 2002).

20. Eidintas, *Lithuanian Emigration to the United States*, 61.

21. William Wolkovich-Valkavicius, "Immigrant Population Patterns of Finns, Estonians, Latvians, and Lithuanians in the U.S. Federal Census of 1930," *Lituanus* 29, no. 1 (1983), www.lituanus.org/1983_1/83_1_02.htm (accessed July 18 2002).

22. Eidintas, *Lithuanian Emigration to the United States*, 61.

23. Ibid., 63.

24. Frederick Taylor was a late-nineteenth-century and early-twentieth-century American thinker who popularized the idea of breaking manual labor into its separate components, and then having each component worked on by a single worker. This increased efficiency and therefore increased production and,

theoretically, profits as well. The assembly line would be a good example of the concept. This work was extremely boring and left for the uneducated masses.

25. "Employees, Highland Park, Ford Motor Co.," in *Telling Detroit's Story*, 194.

26. "Selected Population Data for Detroit and Michigan," in *Telling Detroit's Story*, 191.

27. Gavrilovich and McGraw, *Detroit Almanac*, 166.

28. "Employees, Highland Park, Ford Motor Co.," 194.

29. Greene, *For God and Country*, 145; See also Antanas Kučas, *Lithuanians in America*, trans. Joseph Boley (Boston: Encyclopedia Lituanica, 1975), 62.

30. Greene, *For God and Country*, 155.

31. Kučas, *Lithuanians in America*, 53.

32. Anthony Dainius, "St. George's Lithuanian Parish," *Dievo Apvaizdos Lietuvių Parapija, 1908-1973*, ed. Jonas Urbonas (Southfield, Mich.: Dievo Apvaizdos lietuvių parapija, 1973), 21.

33. Stasys Garliauskas, ed., *Šv. Antano Parapija: Auksinio Jubiliejaus Sukaktivinis Leidinys, 1920-1970* (Detroit, Mich.: Šv. Antano [lietuvių] parapija, 1970), 10-14.

34. Kučas, *Lithuanians in America*, 53.

35. Prutenis, "Orchard Lake," *Lietuvių Enciklopedija*, vol. 10, ed. J. Girnius (South Boston, Mass.: Lietuvių enciklopedijos leidykla, 1960), 163. See also: Garliauskas, *Šv. Antano Parapija*, 114.

36. Gillis, *Growing Up in Old Lithuanian Town*, 5.

37. Ibid.

38. Ibid., 6.

39. Ibid., 86.

40. Rasa Karvelienė, ed., *Dievo Apvaizdo Lietuvių Parapija, 1908-1998* (Southfield, Mich.: Dievo Apvaizdo lietuvių parapija, 1998), 57.

41. Knights of Lithuania Homepage: http://www.knightsoflithuania.com/.

42. Kučas, *Lithuanians in America*, 96.

43. Ibid., 132.

44. Antanas Kučas, *Lietuvių Romos Katalikų Susivienijimas Amerikoje* (Wilkes-Barre, Penn.: "Garso," 1956), 124.

45. Kučas, *Lithuanians in America*, 124.

46. Kučas, *Lietuvių Romos Katalikų Susivienijimas Amerikoje*, 252.

47. Kučas, *Lithuanians in America*, 281.

48. *Septintasis Amerikos Lietuvių Kongresas, Detroite, 1969m* (Chicago: n.p., 1969), iv-v.

49. Kučas, *Lietuvių Romos Katalikų Susivienijimas Amerikoje*, 86–87.

50. Jessie Ecker Daraska, "Lithuanians in Michigan," *Genealogija* 7, no. 1 (1996): 4–5.

51. Gillis, *Growing Up in Old Lithuanian Town*, 5; Also confirmed by an interview with Shannon Andrulis-Thomas.

52. Simutis, *Pasaulio Lietuvių Žinynas*, 302.

53. "Michigan Cemetery Records," Lithuanian Global Genealogical Society, www. angelfire.com/ut/Luthuanian (accessed August 13, 2002).

54. Frank Passic, "Lithuanians in Albion, Michigan," www.albionmich.com/ history/histor_notebook/S_Lith.shtml (accessed August 13, 2002).

55. Clarence J. Monette, *Painesdale, Michigan: Old and New* (Lake Linden, Mich.: Clarence J. Monette, 1983), 68.

56. Russell M. Magnaghi, letter to author, January 12, 2002.

57. Gillis, *Growing Up in Old Lithuanian Town*, 63.

58. Kastytis Giedraitis, "Detroito Sporto Klubas 'Kovas,'" in *Dievo Apvaizdo Lietuvių Parapija, 1908–1998*, 76–77.

59. Gillis, *Growing Up in Old Lithuanian Town*, 65–69.

60. Antanas J. Van Reenan, *Lithuanian Diaspora: Konigsberg to Chicago* (Lanham, Md.: University of America, 1990), 107.

61. According to statistical data, 760,058 exiles lived in all three occupation zones in West Germany beginning in 1946: 94,730 were Latvians and 30,978 were Estonians, along with the Lithuanians. (Eidintas, *Lithuanian Emigration to the United States*, 212–13). Apparently, Lithuanians were not the only ones afraid of the Soviet government.

62. Vaclovas Čižiūnas and Simas Sužiedelis, "Švietimas Nepriklausomojoje Lietuvoje," *Lietuvių Enciklopedija: Lietuva*, vol. 15 (South Boston, Mass.: Lietuvių enciklopedijos leidykla, 1968), 770.

63. As a youth camper at Camp Dainava, the author remembers every day ending with a song sung by memory by the whole camp, from second-graders to the retired-aged cooks. The song title was "The Birds Return Home." "Birds" were symbolic of the exiled Lithuanians and "home" symbolized Lithuania.

64. Van Reenan, *Lithuanian Diaspora*, 142.

65. Camp Pilėnai was created by the Lithuanian National Guard in exile and Camp Rakas was created by the Lithuanian Boy and Girl Scouts.

66. Vacys Rociūnas, ed. *Dainava 25* (Brooklyn, N.Y.: Franciscan Press, 1981), 6.

67. Bishop Zaleski was a professor at St. Mary's College and S.S. Cyril and Metho-

dius Seminary in Orchard Lake in the 1930s. He became the second bishop of Lansing in 1965, which is important to note, because Camp Dainava was within the Lansing Diocese's jurisdiction by then (www.dioceseoflansing.org/bishop/history.html).

68. Van Reenan, *Lithuanian Diaspora*, 207–10.

69. Pranas Zaranka, ed., *ALRKF Jaunimo Stovyklos Informacinis Leidinys, 1959 m.* (Putnam, Conn.: Immaculata Press, 1959), 8.

70. Rociūnas, *Dainava 25*, 70.

71. *ALRKF Jaunimo Stovyklos Informacinis Leidinys, 1956–58 m.* (Putnam, Conn.: Immaculata Press, 1958), 4–5.

72. Fr. Yla was sent to the Nazi concentration camp Stutthof during the Nazi occupation of Lithuania. He wrote a memoir of that experience, *A Priest in Stutthof: Human Experiences in the World of the Subhuman*. He died in 1983.

73. Ingrida Korsakienė, ed., *Heritage in Your Pocket 2003* (Manchester, Mich.: Dainava "HIYP," 2003), 2.

74. Kučas, *Lithuanians in America*, 212.

75. Pranas Zaranka . . . *iš praeities* . . . *Detroito lituanistinių mokyklų veiklos atspindžiai penktan dešimtin žengiant, 1949–1990* (N.p., 1990), 2–3. No date is given for the final year of this school but it closed as less students attended. Some joined the Knights. Garliauskas, *Šv. Antano Parapija*, 68.

76. Zaranka, . . . *iš praeities* . . . *Detroito lituanistinių mokyklų veiklos atspindžiai penktan dešimtin žengiant*, 4.

77. Kučas, *Lithuanians in America*, 213.

78. Zaranka, . . . *iš praeities* . . . *Detroito lituanistinių mokyklų veiklos atspindžiai penktan dešimtin žengiant*, 4–6.

79. Ibid., 7.

80. Karvelienė, *Dievo Apvaizdo Lietuvių Parapija*, 82–83.

81. Kučas, *Lithuanians in America*, 291–93.

82. Raugas, *JAV LB Trys Dešimtmečiai*, 337.

83. Michigan Republican Party website: www.migop.org/leadership/chair.asp (accessed May 13, 2005).

84. Violeta Abarius, interview by author, Ann Arbor, Michigan, August 8, 2002.

85. The author had just served his first summer season as administrator of Camp Dainava. The last day of the summer camping season had just ended when we heard the news of U.S. recognition. Andrius Viskantas broke open a bottle of champagne to celebrate.

86. The author was riding on a bus through Vilnius in 1989 when he saw a sign labeled "Teniso Kortai." Take the endings off the words, one can make out the phonetic equivalent for "Tennis Court." The author's third-wave sensibilities about the Lithuanian language and its static existence were destroyed.

87. Ingrida, "Emigranto Laiškas," *Ateitis* 89, no. 1 (2002): 14–15.

88. Gintaras Karaitis, interview by author, Chikaming Township (near Union Pier), Michigan, July 15, 2002.

89. Viktoria Juodgudis and Milda Rudaitis, "Tauto Pažinimo Stovyklėle Union Pier," *Draugas*, September 26, 2002, 6.

90. Karaitis, interview by author; Milda Rudaitis, interview by author, Union Pier, Michigan, July 15, 2002.

91. Rudaitis, interview by author.

92. "Michigan Cemetery Records," Lithuanian Global Genealogical Society, www. angelfire.com/ut/Luthuanian (accessed August 13, 2002).

93. Karvelienė, *Dievo Apvaizdo Lietuvių Parapija*, 25–26.

For Further Reference

Abarius, Mykolas. Interview by the author. Livonia, Michigan, August 11, 2002.

Abarius, Violeta. Interview by the author. Ann Arbor, Michigan, August 8, 2002.

Alisauskas, Arunas. "Lithuanians." In *Harvard Encyclopedia of American Ethnic Groups*, edited by Stephen Thornstrom. Cambridge, Mass.: Belknap, 1980.

Allen, James Paul, and Eugene James Turner. *We the People: An Atlas of America's Ethnic Diversity*. New York: MacMillan, 1988.

ALRKF Jaunimo Stovyklos Informacinis Leidinys, 1956–58 m. Putnam, Conn.: Immaculata Press, 1958.

Andrulis-Thomas, Shannon. Interview by the author. Cadillac, Michigan, July 12, 2002.

"The Baltic Caucus: U.S. House of Representatives." Www.house.gov/shimkus/baltic/baltic.shtml (accessed July 31, 2005).

Budreckis, Algirdas M., ed. *The Lithuanians in America, 1651–1975: A Chronology and Fact Book*. Dobbs Ferry, N.Y.: Oceana Publications, 1976.

Čižiūnas, Vaclovas, and Simas Sužiedelis. "Švietimas Nepriklausomojoje Lietuvoje." In *Lietuvių Enciklopedija: Lieutva*, vol. 15. South Boston, Mass.: Lietuvių enciklopedijos leidykla, 1968.

Dainius, Anthony. "St. George's Lithuanian Parish." In *Dievo Apvaizdos Lietuvių Parapija, 1908–1973*, edited by Jonas Urbonas. Southfield, Mich.: Dievo Apvaizdos lietuvių parapija, 1973.

Daraska, Jessie Ecker. "Lithuanians in Michigan." *Genealogija* 7, no. 1 (1996): 4-5.

Dumpys, Bishop Hans G. E-mail to author, July 18, 2003.

Dunbar, Willis F., and George S. May. *Michigan: A History of the Wolverine State*. 3rd ed. Grand Rapids, Mich.: Eerdmans, 1995.

Eidintas, Alfonsas. *Lithuanian Emigration to the United States: 1868-1950*, translated by Thomas A. Michalski. Vilnius, Lithuania: Mokslo ir enciklopediju leidybos institutas, 2003.

"Employees, Highland Park, Ford Motor Co." In *Telling Detroit's Story*. Detroit: Detroit 300, 2001, 194.

Fainhauz, David. *Lithuanians in the USA: Aspects of Ethnic Identity*, translated by Algirdas Dumcius. Chicago: Library Press, 1991.

Fountain Celebrates 100 Years. Fountain, Mich.: Fountain Village Council and Fountain Chamber of Commerce, 1983.

Fuller, George N. *Michigan: A Centennial History of the State and Its People*, vol. 2. Chicago: Lewis Publishing Company, 1939.

Garliauskas, Stasys, ed. *Šv. Antano Parapija: Auksinio Jubiliejaus Sukaktivinis Leidinys, 1920-1970*. Detroit, Mich.: Sv. Antano (lietuvių) parapija, 1970.

Gavrilovich, Peter, and Bill McGraw, eds. *The Detroit Almanac: 300 Years of Life in the Motor City*. Detroit, Mich.: Detroit Free Press, 2001.

Gedmintas, Aleksandras. *An Interesting Bit of Identity: The Dynamics of Ethnic Identity in a Lithuanian-American Community*. New York: AMS Press, 1989.

Gerutis, Albertas, ed. *Lithuania: 700 Years*, translated by Algirdas Budreckis. New York: Manyland Books, 1969.

Giedraitis, Kastytis. "Detroito Sporto Klubas 'Kovas.'" In *Dievo Apvaizdo Lietuvių Parapija, 1908-1998*, edited by Rasas Karvelienė, 76-77. Southfield, Mich.: Dievo Apvaizdo lietuvių parapija, 1998.

Gillis, Edward V. *Growing Up in Old Lithuanian Town*. Grand Rapids, Mich.: Grand Rapids Historical Commission, 2001.

Greene, Victor. *For God and Country: The Rise of Polish and Lithuanian Ethnic Consciousness in America, 1860-1910*. Madison: State Historical Society of Wisconsin, 1975.

Grigaitis, Albinas. Interview by the author. Livonia, Michigan, August 5, 2002.

Gureckas, Algimantas. "The Social and Political Activity of the Lithuanian Emigration." *Baltic Forum* 2, no. 2 (1985): 16-26.

Harrison, E. J., ed. *Lithuania 1928*. London: Hazell, Watson and Viney, 1928.

Hartman, Gary. "Building the Ideal Immigrant: Reconciling Lithuanianism and 100 Percent Americanism to Create a Respectable Nationalist Movement, 1870–1922." *Journal of American Ethnic History* 18, no. 1 (1998): 36–76.

———. "Dollars, Diplomacy and Dignity: United States Economic Involvement in Lithuania, 1914–1940." *Journal of Baltic Studies* 28, no. 2, (1997): 153–70.

Hill, C. Warner Vander. *Settling the Great Lakes Frontier: Immigration to Michigan, 1837–1924*. Lansing: Michigan Historical Commission, 1970.

Ingrida. "Emigranto Laiškas" *Ateitis,* 89, no. 1 (2002): 14–15.

Jakštas, Juozas. "Lietuviai Užsienyje." In *Lietuvių Enciklopedija, Vol. 15, Lietuvių,* edited by Vincas Maciūnas. South Boston, Mass.: Lietuvių enciklopedijos leidykla, 1968.

Jonaitis, Vytautas. Interview by the author. Grand Rapids, Michigan, July 14, 2002.

———. LB Grand Rapids Apylinkos Istorijos: Antra Dalis. Unpublished.

Juodgudis, Viktoria, and Milda Rudaitis. "Tauto Pažinimo Stovyklėlė Union Pier." *Draugas,* September 26, 2002, 6.

Karaitis, Gintaras. Interview by the author. Chikaming Township (near Union Pier), Michigan, July 15, 2002.

Karvelienė, Rasa, ed. *Dievo Apvaizdo Lietuvių Parapija, 1908–1998.* Southfield, Mich.: Dievo Apvaizdo lietuvių parapija, 1998.

———. *Gabija ir Baltija-50 or Gabijos ir Baltijos Skaučių ir Skautų Tuntai: 1950–2000.* Southfield, Mich.: Gabijos is Baltijos tuntai Detroite, 2000.

Kavaliunas, John. "Lithuanian-American Population Growing, Becoming More Geographically Dispersed." *Lituanus* 42, no. 2 (1994): 9–14.

Klevorn, Patti. "Tradition: Fountain Family Continues Making Farmer's Cheese Old Country Style." *Ludington Daily News,* October 20, 2001, A1 and A3.

"The Knights of Lithuania Homepage." www.knightsoflithuania.com/ (accessed January 2, 2004).

Korsakienė, Ingrida, ed. *Heritage in Your Pocket, 2003.* Manchester, Mich.: Dainava "HIYP," 2003.

Krisciunas, Raymond G. "The Emigrant Experience: The Decision of Lithuanian Refugees to Emigrate, 1945–1950." *Lituanus* 29, no. 2 (1983): 30–39.

Kromkowski, John. "Immigration, Ethnicity and the Neighborhood Agenda: Urbanization in America." www.crvp.org/book/Serie07/1-5/chapter_xviii.htm (accessed July 11, 2003).

Kučas, Antanas. *Lietuvių Romos Katalikų Susivienijimas Amerikoje.* Wilkes-Barre, Pa.: "Garso," 1956.

———. *Lithuanians in America,* translated by Joseph Boley. Boston, Mass.: Encyclopedia Lituanica, 1975.

"Lithuanian Freedom Cemetry, Grand Rapids, Michigan, USA." Compiled by George Rodgers. Lithuanian Global Genealogical Society, 1999. www.angelfire.com/ut/Luthuanian/markers.html (accessed August 13, 2002).

Lukosevičius, L., and R. Sinkūnas. *Mokyklinis Lietuvos Istorijos Atlasas V-X klasems.* Vilnius, Lithuania: Pradai, 1993.

Magnaghi, Russell M. Letter to author, January 12, 2002.

Majauskas, Donna. "1993 American-Lithuanian Disability Rehabilitation Exchange Program." *Lituanus* 42, no. 2 (1994): 72–77.

"Michigan Cemetery Records." Compiled by George Rogers. Lithuanian Global Genealogical Society, 1999. www.angelfire.com/ut/Luthuanian (accessed August 13, 2002).

"Michigan GOP Chairman Saul Anuzis." Michigan Republican Party, 1998–2005. www.migop.org/leadership/chair.asp (accessed May 13, 2005).

Monette, Clarence J. *Painesdale, Michigan: Old and New.* Lake Linden, Mich.: Clarence J. Monette, 1983.

Nakas, Alfonsas. "Detroit." In *Encyclopedia Lituanica, vol. 2,* edited by Simas Suziedelis 58–62. Boston, Mass.: Juozas Kapocius, 1972.

1979 World Lithuanian Roman Catholic Directory. N.p., Camp Dainava Library.

"1920 Michigan Census." Lithuanian Global Genealogical Society, www.angelfire.com/mi/lithgen/1920.html (accessed August 13, 2002).

Passic, Frank. "Detroit, Michigan 'Lithuanian Lunch' Token." *Knight* 24, no.1 (2002): 3.

———. "Lithuanian Tokens of Grand Rapids, Michigan." *Knight* 23, no.5 (2001): 1–2.

———. "Lithuanians in Albion, Michigan." www.albionmich.com/history/histor_notebook/S_Lith.shtml (accessed August 13, 2002).

Pauža, Vl. "Detroitas." In *Lietuvių Enciklopedija, vol. 4,* edited by Vaclovas Biržiška, 473–78. South Boston, Mass.: Lietuvių enciklopedijos leidykla, 1954.

Plateris, Aleksandras. "Occupational Adjustment of Professional Refugees: A Case Study of Lithuanian Professionals in the United States." *Lituanus* 10, no. 3/4 (1964): 27–44.

Polikaitis, Audrius. Interview by the author. Camp Dainava, Manchester, Michigan, August 6, 2002.

Prutenis. "Orchard Lake." In *Lietuvių Enciklopedija, vol. 21,* edited by J. Girnius, 163. S. Boston, Mass.: Lietuvių enciklopedijos leidykla, 1960. (Based on *S. S. Kiriliaus ir Metodijaus seminarija Amerikos lietuvių katalikų metraštis, 1916.*)

Radžius, Vytautas. *Trečioji Šokių Šventė*. Chicago: n.p., 1968.

Raugas, Balys, ed. *JAV LB Trys Dešimtmečiai*. Jungtinių Amerikos Valstybių Lietuvių Bendruomenės Krašto Valdyba, 1982.

Rociūnas, Vacys, ed. *Dainava 25*. Brooklyn, N.Y.: Franciscan Press, 1981.

———. *Dainava, 1955–1975*. Brooklyn, N.Y.: Franciscan Press, 1975.

Rohozinska, Joanna. "The Conquest of Pragmatism: A New Chapter in Polish-Lithuanian Relation." *Central Europe Review* 1, no. 13 (September 13, 1999).

Rudaitis, Milda. Interview by the author. Union Pier, Michigan, July 15, 2002.

"St. George's Church Membership List, Saginaw, Michigan, 1918–1931." Lithuanian Global Resources, 1998. www.angelfire.com/mi/lithgen/saginawa2c.html (accessed August 13, 2002).

S. S. Peter and Paul Church: 1904–1979: 75th Anniversary. Grand Rapids, Mich.: N.p.

"Selected Population Data for Detroit and Michigan." In *Telling Detroit's Story*, 191. Detroit: Detroit 300, 2001.

Senn, Alfred Erich, and Alfonsas Eidintas. "Lithuanian Immigrants in America and the Lithuanian National Movement before 1914." *Journal of American Ethnic History* 6, no. 2 (1987): 5–19.

Septintasis Amerikos Lietuvių Kongresas, Detroite, 1969m. Chicago: n.p., 1969.

Sienkiewicz, Henryk. *The Teutonic Knights*, translated by Bernard W. A. Massey, edited by Miroslav Lipinski. 1900; New York: Hippocrene Books, 1993.

Simutis, Anicetas, ed. *Pasaulio Lietuvių Žinynas* [Lithuanian World Directory]. New York: Lithuanian Chamber of Commerce, 1953.

———. *Pasaulio Lietuvių Žinynas* [Lithuanian World Directory]. New York: Lithuanian Chamber of Commerce, 1958.

Shurtliff, Janet LaBeau. "Dainava: Lithuanian Camp on W. Austin Road." *Manchester Journal*, May 1990, 3–5.

Sukauskas, Antanas, Antanas Vaitenas, and Antanas Grinius, eds. *Detroito Švyturio Jūrų Šaulių 15-tos Metų Sukaktis: 1967–1982*. Detroit: Švyturio Jūrų Šaulių kuopa, 1982.

Urbonas, Jonas, ed. *Dievo Apvaizdo Lietuvių Parapija, 1908–1973*. Southfield, Mich.: Dievo Apvaizdos lietuvių parapija, 1973.

———. "Lithuanians." In *The Peoples of Michigan Series: Vol. 2: Ethnic Groups in Michigan*. Detroit, Mich.: Michigan Ethnic Heritage Center and University of Michigan Ethnic Studies Program, 1983.

Van Reenan, Antanas J. *Lithuanian Diaspora: Konigsberg to Chicago*. Lanham, Md.: University of America, 1990.

Wolkovich-Valkavicius, William. "Immigrant Population Patterns of Finns, Estonians, Latvians, and Lithuanians in the U.S. Federal Census of 1930." *Lituanus* 29, no. 1 (1983).

———. "Immigrants Who Became Lithuanian by Becoming American." *Lituanus* 42, no. 2 (1994): 58–71.

Zaranka, Pranas. *ALRKF Jaunimo Stovyklos Informacinis Leidinys, 1959 m.* Putnam, Conn.: Immaculata Press, 1959.

———. *. . . . iš praeities . . . Detroito lituanistinių mokyklų veiklos atspindžiai penktan dešimtin žengiant, 1949–1990.* N.p., 1990.

Index

A

Abarius, Mykolas, 49

Abarius, Violeta, 61

Adamkus, Valdas, 41, 67, 68

Adams Township (Mich.), 37

Albion (Mich.), 33–35, 74

Albion Malleable Iron Co., 33

Alger County (Mich.), 36

American-Lithuanian Disability and
Rehabilitation Exchange Program,
78

Andrulis, Allen, 33

Andrulis, Angelė, 33

Andrulis, Jonas, 33

Andrulis Dairy Farm (Michigan Farm
Cheese Dairy), 32, 33

Anužis, Saulius, 60

Ateitininkai, *see* Ateitis

Ateitis (organization), 47, 49, 51, 52, 56

Ateitis (magazine), 69

Audinys, 58, 59

Aušra (Saturday school), 54, 55

B

Bachelor (Mich.), 32

Bachunas, Juozas, 67

Baltic (Mich.), 35

Baltic Caucus, 59, 60

Baltic Sea, 3, 48

Baltija (Detroit Lith. Boy Scouts), 56

Banionytė, Asta, 61

basketball, 39–42

Bendoraitis, Motiejus, 20

Beverly Shores (Ind.), 71

book smugglers, 6

Boreišis, Ignas, 20, 21, 23, 53, 54

Bremen (Germany), 8

Brooklyn (N.Y.), 28

Butkus, Dick, 43

C

Catholic University of America, 24

Cedarville (Mich.), 35

Chicago, 18, 47, 49, 67, 71; Lith.
    conventions and organizations in,
    27, 28, 30, 41, 59; Lith. population
    in, 2, 12; transplants from, in
    Michigan, 14, 33, 35, 72

Chippewa County (Mich.), 36

Christian Democratic Party (Lith.), 56

Cicero (Ill.), 33

Čičinskas, 1, 45, 46

Civilian Conservation Corps (CCC), 34

Čižauskas, Juozas, 23

Cleveland (Ohio), 27, 47, 49

coal mining, 13, 30

Communist Party of America, 28

conscription, 5, 11

Copper Country, 35

copper mining, 12, 13

country of origin, 7, 8

culture, 17

Custer (Mich.), 32, 48

D

Dabrowski, Jozef, 20

Dabušis, Viktoras, 76

Daggett (Mich.), 35

Dainava (camp), 26, 47–52, 58, 76

Daley, Richard, 29

Damušienė, Jadvyga, 49, 51, 60

Damušis, Adolfas, 48, 49, 60

Damušytė, Gintė, 60, 61

Darbininkas (N.Y.), 19

Dayton (Ohio), 27

Deimanta, V., 28

Democratic affiliation, 27, 30, 57, 59

Detroit: assimilation in, 77, 78; and
    Camp Dainava, 47, 49, 76; fifth
    wave in, 75; fourth wave in, 63;
    Jews in, 36; Lith. organizations
    in, 25–30, 56, 58; Lith. population
    in, 12, 74; Lith. Saturday School
    in, 53–54; Michigan Farm Cheese
    Dairy in, 33; parishes in, 17, 19, 20,
    23, 31, 74; political work in, 59–61;
    sports in, 39–42; work and wages
    in, 12, 14, 15

Dexnis, Anthony, 23

displaced persons, 26, 45, 46, 47, 48, 50,
    52, 58, 63, 76

Displaced Persons Act of 1948, 45

Divine Providence (Lith.) parish
    (Southfield, Mich.), 23, 26, 29, 40,
    55, 60, 74, 76

Draugas (Chicago), 19

F

Festival of the Forks, 35

Fines, Abraham, 36

Fines, Joseph, 36

Foley, John, 19

Ford Motor Company, 12, 15, 19, 20, 38

Fountain (Mich.), 32

Free Soil (Mich.), 32

French Teachers' Association, 52

Frontininkai, 51

G

Gabija (Detroit Lith. Girl Scouts), 56

Galinis, Louis, 9

Gallagher, Michael, 19, 20

Germany, 8, 54

Getz, Louis, 36, 37

Getz Department Store, 37

Gillis, Edward, 9

Gobienė, Galina, 58–59

Gogebic County (Mich.), 37

Grand Rapids: assimilation in, 74; effects of suburbanization in, 31; first Lithuanians in, 9; Lith. parish in, 17, 21–23; Lith. organizations in, 24, 25, 27, 28, 58; Lith. Saturday school in, 53; sports in, 39, 43; work and wages in, 12, 14

guberniyas (governing districts), 11

H

Hamburg-America Line, 8

Harding, William, 31

Heritage Camp, *47, 50,* 51, 52, 72, 76

Holy Family Parish (South Range, Mich.), 35, 36

Houghton (Mich.), 12

Houghton County (Mich.), 37

I

Ilgauskas, Šarūnas, 41

immigration officials, 8

Indo-European family of languages, 5

Irons (Mich.), 32

Isle Royale (Mich.), 34

J

Jackson (Mich.), 33, 74

Jaksztys, Stanislaus, 35

Jasėnas, Albert, 34

Jews, 11, 33, 36, 71, 73

Jogaila, King, 4

Johnson Manufacturing Co., 34

Jurevicius, Joe, 43

Juška, Antanas, 49

K

Kalėdos Eglutė, 53

Karaitis, Gintaras, 71

Kasputienė, Rusnė, 58–59

Kaupas, Antanas, 14, 20, 21

Kazukio mugė, 56

Kemėšis, Fabian, 19, 26

KGB (Soviet Secret Police), 63

Kiedis, Anton, 32

Kingsford (Mich.), 38

Knights of Lithuania (Vyčiai), 27, 31, 51, 54; Adopt a Lithuanian Seminarian, 26; Aid to Lithuania, Inc., 26; Local Council 79 (Detroit), 19, 26; Local Council 102 (Detroit), 26

Kolesinskis, George, 18

Kovas (athletic club; Detroit), 40–42

Kriaučiūnas, Matas, 18

Kriščiunevičius, Viktoras, 74

Kudirka, Vincas, 54

L

Lake County (Mich.), 32, 33, 74

Lansing (Mich.), 60

Lapelis, Petras, 21

Latin alphabet, 5, 6

Latvia, 3, 7

Lemont (Ill.), 72

Lipkus, Joseph, 22, 23, 24

Lithuania, 2–6, 11, 29, 46, 53, 57, 65, 78

Lithuanian Alliance of America (SLA),

27, 28

Lithuanian American Community
(JAVLB), 57, 58, 60

Lithuanian American Council (ALTas),
29

Lithuanian American Roman Catholic
Federation Camp Dainava, 26,
47–52, 58, 76

Lithuanian American Roman Catholic
Women's Alliance, 24; Chapter
42 (Grand Rapids), 25; Chapter 51
(Detroit), 25; Chapter 54 (Detroit),
25; Chapter 64 (Detroit) 25

Lithuanian American Roman Catholic
Youth Camps, 48

Lithuanian Athletic Club (Grand
Rapids), 39

Lithuanian Community (LB), 53, 54,
58, 61; Cultural Fund, 58; Cultural
Information Bureau, 58; Education
Council, 58

Lithuanian Community Detroit Area
Lithuanian School, 55

Lithuanian Council, 28

Lithuanian Cultural Center (Southfield,
Mich.), 1, 40, 55, 56, 60, 61

Lithuanian Education Association of
South Redford, 55

Lithuanian embassy, 61

Lithuanian Folk Dance Festival, 53, 58,
59

Lithuanian Folk Dancing Teachers'
Organization, 51

Lithuanian Hope Society, 21

Lithuanian Information Center, 60

Lithuanian Nationalist Association of

America, 28

Lithuanian Nationalist "Sandara"
Association, 27, 28, 67

Lithuanian Pedagogical Institute
(Chicago), 73

Lithuanian Pontifical College (Rome),
26

Lithuanian Roman Catholic Alliance of
America (LRKSA), 27, 28, 31: Lodge
190 (Detroit), 19

Lithuanian Roman Catholic Federation
of America, 27, 48

Lithuanian Saturday schools, 1, 47, 52,
53, 54, 55, 58, 68, 72

Lithuanian Socialist Alliance, 28

Lithuanian Socialist Party of America, 28

Lithuanian Song Festival, 53, 58

Lithuanian Students' St. Casimir's
Society at the Polish Seminary, 21

Lithuanian Teachers' Association, 51, 54

Lithuanian World Community (PLB),
57, 58

Lowenstein, Samuel, 36

M

Mackinac County (Mich.), 25

Madison Square Gardens (N.Y.), 28

Maironis, 1, 6

Manchester (Mich.), 48

Marenisco (Mich.), 37

Marquette (Mich.), 36, 37

Marquette Diocese (Mich.), 24

Marquette Park (Chicago), 73

Mason County (Mich.), 32, 33, 74

Matulaitis, Wenceslaus, 22

McMeis, John, 37–38

Menominee County (Mich.), 35

Michigan Farm Cheese Dairy (Andrulis

    Dairy Farm), 32, 33

Mickus, Andrew, 37

Mikolainis, P., 28

Milda's Corner Store, 73

Morton West High School (Berwyn,

    Ill.), 73

Pennsylvania, 2, 12, 14, 18, 24, 28, 30, 43

Petraitis, Augustus, 21

Pilėnai (camp in Manchester, Mich.),

    47, 76

Poland, 3, 7

Polish-Lithuanian Alliance, 4

Ponganis, Simon, 22

Prussia, 3, 7, 8

N

Nadeau (Mich.), 35

Nakas, Viktoras, 61

Nationalist Party (Lith.), 56, 67

Naujoji Lietuva (New Lithuania), 14,

    32, 48

Nemunas River, 3, 6

New York (City), 14, 33

New York LAK (Lietuvių Atletų Klubas),

    41

North Atlantic Treaty Organization

    (NATO), 60, 78

North German Lloyd, 8

O

Oberlin College, 61

Oklahoma City, 23, 24

Olišauskas, Antanas, 14, 18

Ontonogan County (Mich.), 37

Orchard Lake (Mich.), 20, 21

P

Painesdale (Mich.), 35, 36, 37, 74

Paradise, Maurice, 37

Passic, Frank, 33, 35

Pauražienė, Elzbieta, 29

Peacock (Mich.), 32

R

Rakas (camp in Custer, Mich.), 48

Redford (Mich.), 54, 55

Refugee Act of 1953, 45

Republican affiliation, 27, 30, 57, 60

Resort Gintaras, 71, 72

Riegle, Donald, Jr., 61

Roman Catholic Church, 17, 27

Roosevelt, Franklin D., 29, 31, 57

Rudaitis, Milda, 73

Russia, Empire of, 5, 7, 12, 14

S

Sabonis, Arvydas, 41

Saginaw (Mich.), 74

St. Adalbert's Parish (Grand Rapids),

    21, 22

St. Albertus' (Polish) Parish (Detroit), 18

St. Anthony (Lith.) Parish (Detroit), 20,

    23, 25, 53, 54, 74

St. Anthony's Society (Detroit), 19, 20

St. Casimir, 26

St. Casimir's Society, 21

St. Casimir's Society of Science, 20

St. George (Lith.) Parish (Detroit), 18, 20,

    23, 25, 39, 53

St. George's Society (Detroit), 18, 23, 25

St. John Nepomucene's (Bohemian)
Parish, 20
St. Joseph's Seminary (Grand Rapids),
24
St. Josephat (Polish) Church (Detroit), 18
St. Mary's (German) Parish (Grand
Rapids), 21–22
St. Mary's (Lith.) Parish (Custer, Mich.),
33
St. Peter's (Lith.) Parish, 20, 74
S.S. Cyril and Methodius Seminary, 20
S.S. Peter and Paul Aid Society, 22, 22, 23
S.S. Peter and Paul (Lith.) Parish (Grand
Rapids), 21–24, 39
Sakocius, Bob, 43
Salatka, Charles A., 24, 42
Šalkauskis, Stasys, 56
Šaltinis, 59
Sandara, 28
Scottville (Mich.), 32
Scouts (Lith.), 47, 51, 56
Shapaila, Ed, 43
Shapaila, Vic, 43
Shapiro, Max, 36
Sharkey, Jack (Juozas Zukauskas), 39
Shimkus, John, 34
Shimkus, John (Rep.), 59
Šilainė, 58
Sisters of the Immaculate Conception of
Mary, 49
Skrypkus, Casimir, 19
Šliupas, Jonas, 14, 18
Smetona, Antanas, 56, 67
Sodus (Mich.), 67
Songaila, Darius, 41
Sons and Daughters of Lithuania Aid

Society, 24, 31
Sons of Lithuania, 35
Southfield (Mich.), 1
South Range (Mich.), 35
South Redford School Board, 55
Soviet Union, 29, 63, 69, 78
Steponas, Darius, 40
svetainė (hall), 24
Szeiva, Vic, 43

T

Tabor Farms, 67
Tannenburg, battle at (1410), 4
Taylor, Frederick, 14, 86–87
Teutonic Order, 3, 4, 5
Third Partition (1795), 5
Thomas, Dan, 33
Thomas, Shannon, 33
Tilžė, 6
Toronto (Canada), 41, 47, 67
Traverse City (Mich.), 28
Truman, Harry S., 57

U

Union of Lublin (1569), 5
Union of Soviet Socialist Republics
(U.S.S.R.), 29, 63, 69, 78
Union Pier (Mich.), 53, 58, 71–74, 75, 78
Unitas, Johnny, 43
United Lithuanian Relief Fund, 29
United States, 6, 7, 9, 10, 11, 46, 68
United States Census, 1920, 7, 10, 36;
1930, 14, 35, 36, 37
University of Michigan, 41, 61
Upper Peninsula (Mich.), 24, 35–38
Urbonas, Jonas, 60

V

Valaitis, Casimir, 18, 19, 20

Valdemaras, Valdas, 75

Vandenberg Public Elementary School, 54, 55

Vasario 16-ta (Lith.) High School (Germany), 73

Vilnius University, 5

Viskantienė, Viktorija, 59

Volskis, Aloyzas, 75

Vytautas Aid Society, 24

Vytautas (Witold) the Great, 3, 4

W

Washington, D.C., 61

"waynians," 68

Weiss, Abe, 36

Western High School (Detroit), 55

West Germany, 46, 47

West Side Beer Distributing, 43

Wilkes-Barre (Penn.), 21, 27, 28

Wilson, Woodrow, 28, 31

Wisconsin, 13, 33, 35

World Lithuanian Games, 41, 67

World Lithuanian Youth Congress, 61

World War I, 7, 9, 19, 34

World War II, 34, 40, 45

Y

Yčas, Martynas, 14

Yla, Stasys, 50

Z

Zaleski, 49, 88

Žiburio ("Shining Light") Saturday School, 55

žiurkiakaimo ("rats' village"), 19

Zukaitis, Felix, 43